CIM

PRACTICE & REVISION KIT

Professional Post-graduate Diploma

Managing Marketing Performance

BPP Professional Education
September 2004

First edition September 2004

ISBN 0 7517 1269 8

British Library Cataloguing-in-Publication Data
A catalogue record for this book
is available from the British Library

Published by

BPP Professional Education
Aldine House, Aldine Place
London W12 8AW

www.bpp.com

Printed in Great Britain by W M Print
45-47 Frederick Street
Walsall, West Midlands
WS2 9NE

All our rights reserved. No part of this publication may be reproduced, stored in a retrieval system or transmitted, in any form or by any means, electronic, mechanical, photocopying, recording or otherwise, without the prior written permission of BPP Professional Education.

We are grateful to the Chartered Institute of Marketing for permission to reproduce in this kit the syllabus, the specimen paper and past examination questions. We are also grateful to the Association of Chartered Certified Accountants for permission to reproduce past examination questions. The suggested solutions to past examination questions have been prepared by BPP Professional Education.

Authors

Brian Searle, Rosemary Schofield

Series editor

Paul Brittain

©
BPP Professional Education
2004

Introduction

Page

CONTENTS

Question and answer checklist/index (iv)
    About this kit (vi)
    Revision (vii)
    Question practice (viii)
    Exam technique (ix)
    Approaching mini-cases (xi)
    The exam paper (xiv)
    Syllabus (xv)

QUESTION BANK 3

ANSWER BANK 27

TEST PAPER
    Specimen paper questions 139
    Specimen paper suggested answers 143

TOPIC INDEX 159

ORDER FORM

REVIEW FORM & FREE PRIZE DRAW

Introduction

The headings indicate the main topics of questions, but questions often cover several different topics.

Questions marked by * are **key questions** which we think you must attempt in order to pass the exam. Tick them off on this list as you complete them.

		Marks	Time allocation mins	Page number Question	Answer
PART A: CREATING THE ORGANISATIONAL CONCEPT FOR THE EFFECTIVE IMPLEMENTATION OF STRATEGY					
1	Participation	25	40	3	27
2	Motivation	25	40	3	28
3	New product development team	25	40	3	30
*4	Planning a team	25	40	3	33
*5	Leadership and performance	25	40	3	35
6	Emotional intelligence	25	40	3	37
PART B: MANAGING CHANGE AND INTERNAL MARKETING					
7	Marketing task	25	40	4	39
*8	Champion of change	25	40	4	40
*9	Marketing orientation	25	40	4	42
10	Change and the individual	25	40	4	44
PART C: IMPLEMENTING THE BUSINESS STRATEGY THROUGH MARKETING ACTIVITIES					
*11	Brand stretching	25	40	5	46
12	Integrity	25	40	5	48
13	Hotel company	25	40	5	50
*14	Crisis management	25	40	5	52
*15	Relationship marketing and IT	25	40	5	54
16	Measuring the value of brands	25	40	6	56
17	Shareholder value analysis	25	40	6	58
18	Brand strategies and equity	25	40	6	59
*19	Ethics and social responsibility	25	40	6	61
*20	Service quality	25	40	6	63
21	Push and pull	25	40	6	66

		Marks	Time allocation Mins	Page number Question	Answer
PART D: MANAGEMENT TECHNIQUES FOR MANAGING THE MARKETING FUNCTION					
22	RUS plc	25	40	7	67
23	Great Utility Services Ltd	25	40	7	69
24	Project guide to conferences	25	40	7	71
*25	Creativity and innovation	25	40	8	72
26	Creative people	25	40	8	75
27	Outsourcing marketing activity	25	40	8	77
28	Innovation	25	40	8	78
*29	Planning for growth	25	40	9	81
30	Managing outside suppliers	25	40	9	83
31	Relationship marketing	25	40	9	86
32	Quality management	25	40	9	86
PART E: MEASUREMENT, EVAUATION AND CONTROL					
*33	Expenditure	25	40	9	89
34	Feedback and control systems	25	40	9	91
*35	Balanced scorecard	25	40	10	93
36	Budgeting	25	40	10	95
MINI-CASES					
*37	Royal Shakespeare Company	50	80	10	96
*38	International Sonatas Hotels	50	80	11	100
*39	Family doctor	50	80	12	105
*40	Silvadawn Leisurewear	50	80	14	108
*41	CiniCentre	50	80	15	110
*42	Paperworks	50	80	17	115
*43	Selfridges	50	80	19	120
*44	Woodstock Furniture	50	80	21	125
*45	Campaigns of global pressure	50	80	22	130

Introduction

About this kit

You're taking CIM exams. You're under time pressure to get your exam revision done and you want to pass first time. Could you make better use of your time? Are you sure that your revision is really relevant to the exam you will be facing?

If you use this BPP Practice & Revision Kit you can be sure that the time you spend revising and practising questions is time well spent.

The BPP Practice & Revision Kit: Managing Marketing Performance

The BPP Practice & Revision Kit has been specifically written for the paper by an expert in marketing education.

- We give you a **comprehensive question and answer checklist** so you can see at a glance which are the key questions that we think you should attempt in order to pass the exam, what the mark and time allocations are and when they were set (where this is relevant)
- We offer **vital guidance** on revision, question practice and exam technique
- We show you the **syllabus** and analyse the **Specimen paper**
- We give you a **comprehensive question bank** containing:
    - *Exam-standard questions*
    - *Full suggested answers* - with summaries of the examiner's comments, where possible
- A **Test Paper** consisting of the Specimen paper, again with full suggested answers, for you to attempt just before the real thing
- A **Topic Index** for ready reference

The Study Text: further help from BPP

The core part of BPP's study package is the Study Text. The Study Text features:

- Structured, methodical syllabus coverage
- Lots of case examples from real businesses throughout, to show you how the theory applies in real life
- Action programmes and quizzes so that you can test that you've mastered the theory
- A question and answer bank
- Key concepts and full index

There's an order form at the back of this Kit.

Passcards

BPP passcards enable you to revise at a glance by summarising key revision points in a card format.

Help us to help you

Your feedback will help us improve our study package. Please complete and return the Review Form at the end of this Kit; you will be entered automatically in a Free Prize Draw.

BPP Professional Education
September 2004

To learn more about what BPP has to offer, visit our website: www.bpp.com

Revision

This is a very important time as you approach the exam. You must remember three things.

> **Use time sensibly**
> **Set realistic goals**
> **Believe in yourself**

Use time sensibly

1. **How much study time do you have?** Remember that you must EAT, SLEEP, and of course, RELAX.

2. **How will you split that available time between each subject?** What are your weaker subjects? They need more time.

3. **What is your learning style?** AM/PM? Little and often/long sessions? Evenings/weekends?

4. **Are you taking regular breaks?** Most people absorb more if they do not attempt to study for long uninterrupted periods of time. A five minute break every hour (to make coffee, watch the news headlines) can make all the difference.

5. **Do you have quality study time?** Unplug the phone. Let everybody know that you're studying and shouldn't be disturbed.

Set realistic goals

1. Have you set a **clearly defined objective** for each study period?
2. Is the objective **achievable**?
3. Will you **stick to your plan**? Will you make up for any **lost time**?
4. Are you **rewarding yourself** for your hard work?
5. Are you leading a **healthy lifestyle**?

Believe in yourself

Are you cultivating the right attitude of mind? There is absolutely no reason why you should not pass this exam if you adopt the correct approach.

- **Be confident** – you've passed exams before, you can pass them again
- **Be calm** – plenty of adrenaline but no panicking
- **Be focused** – commit yourself to passing the exam

Introduction

Question practice

Do not simply open this Kit and, beginning with question 1, start attempting all of the questions. You first need to ask yourself three questions.

> **Am I ready to answer questions?**
> **Do I know which questions to do first?**
> **How should I use this Kit?**

Am I ready to answer questions?

1   Check that you are familiar with the material.

2   If you are happy, you can go ahead and start answering questions. If not, go back to your BPP Study Text and revise first.

How should I use this Kit?

1   Once you are confident with the Do you know? checklists and the tutorial questions, you should try as many as possible of the exam-standard questions; at the very least you should attempt the **key questions,** which are highlighted in the **question and answer checklist/index** at the front of the Kit.

2   Try to **produce full answers under timed conditions**; you are practising exam technique as much as knowledge recall here. Don't look at the answer, your BPP Study Text or your notes for any help at all.

3   **Mark your answers to the questions as if you were the examiner**. Only give yourself marks for what you have written, not for what you meant to put down, or would have put down if you had had more time. If you did badly, try another question.

4   Read the **Tutorial notes** in the answers very carefully and take note of the advice given and any **comments by the examiner**.

5   When you have practised the whole syllabus, go back to the areas you had problems with and **practise further questions**.

6   When you feel you have completed your revision of the entire syllabus to your satisfaction, answer the **test your knowledge** quiz. This covers selected areas from the entire syllabus and answering it unseen is a good test of how well you can recall your knowledge of diverse subjects quickly.

7   Finally, when you think you really understand the entire subject, **attempt the test paper** at the end of the Kit. Sit the paper under strict exam conditions, so that you gain experience of selecting and sequencing your questions, and managing your time, as well as of writing answers.

Exam technique

Passing professional examinations is half about having the knowledge, and half about doing yourself full justice in the examination. You must have the right approach to two things.

> **The day of the exam**
> **Your time in the exam hall**

The day of the exam

1   Set at least one alarm (or get an alarm call) for a morning exam.

2   Have something to eat but beware of eating too much; you may feel sleepy if your system is digesting a large meal.

3   Allow plenty of time to get to the exam hall; have your route worked out in advance and listen to news bulletins to check for potential travel problems.

4   Don't forget pens, pencils, rulers, erasers.

5   Put new batteries into your calculator and take a spare set (or a spare calculator).

6   Avoid discussion about the exam with other candidates outside the exam hall.

Your time in the exam hall

1   **Read the instructions (the 'rubric') on the front of the exam paper carefully**

   Check that the exam format hasn't changed. It is surprising how often examiners' reports remark on the number of students who attempt too few – or too many – questions, or who attempt the wrong number of questions from different parts of the paper. Make sure that you are planning to answer the right number of questions.

2   **Select questions carefully**

   Read through the paper once, then quickly jot down key points against each question in a second read through. Select those questions where you could latch on to 'what the question is about' – but remember to check carefully that you have got the right end of the stick before putting pen to paper.

3   **Plan your attack carefully**

   Consider the order in which you are going to tackle questions. It is a good idea to start with your best question to boost your morale and get some easy marks 'in the bag'.

4   **Check the time allocation for each question**

   Each mark carries with it a time allocation of 1.6 minutes (including time for selecting and reading questions). A 20 mark question therefore should be completed in 32 minutes. When time is up, you must go on to the next question or part. Going even one minute over the time allowed brings you a lot closer to failure.

5   **Read the question carefully and plan your answer**

   Read through the question again very carefully when you come to answer it. Plan your answer to ensure that you keep to the point. Two minutes of planning plus eight minutes of writing is virtually certain to earn you more marks than ten minutes of writing.

6 **Produce relevant answers**

Particularly with written answers, make sure you answer the question set, and not the question you would have preferred to have been set.

7 **Gain the easy marks**

Include the obvious if it answers the question and don't try to produce the perfect answer.

Don't get bogged down in small parts of questions. If you find a part of a question difficult, get on with the rest of the question. If you are having problems with something, the chances are that everyone else is too.

8 **Produce an answer in the correct format**

The examiner will state in the requirements the format in which the question should be answered, for example in a report or memorandum.

9 **Follow the examiner's instructions**

You will annoy the examiner if you ignore him or her. The examiner will state whether he or she wishes you to 'discuss', 'comment', 'evaluate' or 'recommend'.

10 **Present a tidy paper**

Students are penalised for poor presentation and so you should make sure that you write legibly, label diagrams clearly and lay out your work neatly. Markers of scripts each have hundreds of papers to mark; a badly written scrawl is unlikely to receive the same attention as a neat and well laid out paper.

11 **Stay until the end of the exam**

Use any spare time checking and rechecking your script.

12 **Don't worry if you feel you have performed badly in the exam**

It is more than likely that the other candidates will have found the exam difficult too. Don't forget that there is a competitive element in these exams. As soon as you get up to leave the exam hall, forget that exam and think about the next – or, if it is the last one, celebrate!

13 **Don't discuss an exam with other candidates**

This is particularly the case if you still have other exams to sit. Even if you have finished, you should put it out of your mind until the day of the results. Forget about exams and relax!

Approaching mini-cases

What is a mini-case?

The mini-case in the examination is a description of an organisation at a moment in time. You first see it in the examination room and so you have 80 minutes to read, understand, analyse and answer the mini-case.

The mini-case (Part A of the paper) carries 50% of the available marks in the examination.

As mini-cases are fundamental to your exam success, you should be absolutely clear about what mini-cases are, the CIM's purpose in using them, and what the examiner seeks; then, in context, you must consider how best they should be tackled.

The purpose of the mini-case

The examiner requires students to demonstrate not only their knowledge of the fundamentals of marketing, but also their ability to use that knowledge in a commercially credible way in the context of a 'real' business scenario.

The examiner's requirements

The examiner is the 'consumer' of your examination script. You should remember first and foremost that a paper is needed which makes his or her life easy. That means that the script should be well laid out, with plenty of white space and neat readable writing. All the basic rules of examination technique discussed earlier must be applied, but because communication skills are fundamental to the marketer, the ability to communicate clearly is particularly important.

An approach to mini-cases

Mini-cases are easy once you have mastered the basic techniques. The key to success lies in adopting a logical sequence of steps which, with practice, you will master. You must enter the exam room with the process as second nature, so you can concentrate your attention on the marketing issues which face you.

Students who are at first apprehensive when faced with a mini-case often come to find them much more stimulating and rewarding than traditional examination questions. There is the added security of knowing that there is no single correct answer to a case study.

Suggested mini-case method

You have about 80 minutes in total.

Introduction

Stage		Minutes
1	Read the mini-case and questions set on it very quickly.	2
2	Read the questions and case again, but carefully. Make brief notes of significant material. Determine key issues in relation to the questions etc.	5
3	Put the case on one side and turn to your notes. What do they contain? A clear picture of the situation? Go back if necessary and concentrate on getting a grip on the scenario outlined.	4
4	Prepare an answer structure plan for question (a) following exactly the structure suggested in the question, highlighting your decisions supported by case data and theory if appropriate. Follow the process outlined for question (b), etc.	3
5	Prepare a timeplan for each part of the question, according to the marks allocated.	1
6	Write your answer	60
7	Read through and correct errors, improve presentation	5
		80

A good answer will be a document on which a competent manager can take action.

Notes

(a) It is not seriously suggested that you can allocate your time quite so rigorously! The purpose of showing detailed timings is to demonstrate the need to move with purpose and control through each stage of the process.

(b) Take time to get the facts into your short term memory. Making decisions is easier once the facts are in your head.

(c) Establish a clear plan and you will find that writing the answers is straightforward.

(d) Some candidates will be writing answers within five minutes. The better candidates will ignore them and concentrate on planning. This is not easy to do, but management of your examination technique is the key to your personal success.

(e) Presentation is crucial. Your answer should be written as a final draft that would go to typing. If the typist could understand every word and replicate the layout, then the examiner will be delighted and it will be marked highly.

Handling an unseen mini-case or caselet in the examination

The following extract is taken from the Chartered Institute of Marketing's Tutor's/Student Guide to the treatment of mini-cases.

Tutor's/Student Guide to the treatment of mini-cases

'It needs to be stated unequivocally that the type of extremely short case (popularly called the mini-case) set in the examinations for Certificate and Diploma subjects cannot be treated in exactly the same way as a long case study issued in advance. If it could there would be little point of going to all the trouble of writing an in-depth case study.

'Far too many students adopt a maxi-case approach using a detailed marketing audit outline which is largely inappropriate to a case consisting only of two or three paragraphs. Others use the SWOT analysis and simply re-write the case under the four headings of strengths, weaknesses, opportunities and threats.

'Some students even go so far as to totally ignore the specific questions set and present a standard maxi-case analysis outline including environmental reviews through to contingency plans.

'The "mini-case" is not really a case at all, it is merely an outline of a given situation, a scenario. Its purpose is to test whether examinees can apply their knowledge of marketing theory and techniques to the company or organisation and the operating environment described in the scenario. For example answers advocating retail audits as part of the marketing information system for a small industrial goods manufacturer demonstrate a lack of practical awareness. Such answers confirm that the examinee has learned a given MIS outline by rote and simply regurgitated this in complete disregard of the scenario. Such an approach would be disastrous in the real world and examinees adopting this approach cannot be passed, ie gain the confidence of the Institute as professional marketing practitioners. The correct approach to the scenario is a mental review of the area covered by the question and the *selection* by the examinee of those particular parts of knowledge or techniques which apply to the case. This implies a rejection of those parts of the student's knowledge which clearly do not apply to the scenario.

'All scenarios are based upon real world companies and situations and are written with a fuller knowledge of how that organisation actually operates in its planning environments. Often the organisation described in the scenario will not be a giant fast moving consumer goods manufacturing and marketing company since this would facilitate mindless regurgitation of textbook outlines and be counter to the intention of this section of the examination.

'More often the scenarios will involve innovative small or medium sized firms which comprise the vast majority of UK companies which lack the resources often assumed by the textbook approach. These firms do have to market within these constraints however and are just as much concerned with marketing communications, marketing planning and control and indeed (proportionately) in international marketing, particularly the Common Market, as are larger enterprises.

'However, as marketing applications develop and expand and as changes take root, the Institute (through its examiners) will wish to test students' knowledge and awareness of these changes and their implication with regard to marketing practice. For example in the public sector increasing attention is being paid to the marketing of leisure services and the concept of "asset marketing" where the "product" is to a greater extent fixed and therefore the option of product as a variable in the marketing mix is somewhat more constrained.

'Tutors and students are referred to Examiners' Reports which repeatedly complain of inappropriateness of answer detail which demonstrates a real lack of *practical* marketing grasp and confirms that a leaned by rote textbook regurgitation is being used. Examples would include:

- The recommendation of national TV advertising for a small industrial company with a local market
- The overnight installation of a marketing department comprising Marketing Director, Marketing Manager, Advertising Manager, Distribution Manager, Sales Manager, etc into what has been described as a very small company
- The inclusion of packaging, branded packs, on-pack offers, etc, in the marketing mix recommendations for a service

'It has to be borne in mind that the award of the Diploma is in a very real sense the granting of a licence to practice marketing and certainly an endorsement of the candidate's practical as well as theoretical grasps of marketing. In these circumstances such treatments of the mini-case as described above cannot be passed and give rise to some concern that perhaps the teaching/learning approach to mini-cases has not been sufficiently differentiated from that recommended for maxi-cases.

'Tutors/distance-learning students are recommended to work on previously set mini-cases and questions and review results against published specimen answers. They are also advised to use course-members' companies/organisations as examples in the constraints/limitations of marketing techniques and how they might need to be modified.

'Students are also advised to answer the specified questions set and if for example a question was on objectives, then undue reference to market analysis and strategies would be treated as extraneous.'

Introduction

The exam paper

Assessment methods and format of the paper

	Marks
Part A: One compulsory question based on an industry scenario or a company mini-case study: this question will be broken down into parts, typically three	50
Part B: Choice of two questions from four	50
	100

The examination will be based on the stated learning outcomes and every examination will cover at least 80% of the syllabus content.

Time allowed: 3 hours

Note: earlier drafts of the assessment methodology for this paper spoke in terms of Parts A, B and C, with one question from a choice of two being answered in each of Parts B and C. This proposal has been superseded by the format described above.

Analysis of Specimen paper

Part A (compulsory)

1 A food processing firm with reputation for high quality, branded producing is in decline. The firm is looking for new opportunities for growth.

    (a) Response to threats
    (b) Choosing a development opportunity

Part B (two from four)

2 Functional interests in mini-case
3 Business case to recruit product manager
4 Balanced scorecard
5 Service quality standards

Syllabus and guidance notes

Aim

The Managing Marketing Performance module covers the implementation of a customer-focussed business strategy in a strategic and global context. It aims to provide participants with the knowledge and skills required to contribute to the successful implementation of a customer-oriented and competitive strategy for the organisation. Its emphasis is on facilitating change in the organisation, ideally towards a stronger market orientation, managing and integrating the marketing function as part of the organisation's response, and measurement.

Related statements of practice

Cd.2 Distil the essence of brands and direct/coordinate a portfolio of brands.

Dd.2 Lead the implementation of the integrated marketing communications strategy.

Ed.2 Direct and maintain competitive product/service portfolios.

Fd.2 Lead the implementation of the strategic and creative use of pricing.

Gd.2 Direct and control support to channel members.

Hd.1 Promote and create a customer orientation and infrastructure for customer relationships.

Hd.2 Direct and control information and activities that deliver customer relationships and service.

Jd.1 Establish and maintain a project management framework in line with strategic objectives.

Jd.2 Direct and control the delivery of programmes and projects.

Kd.1 Establish and promote the use of metrics to improve marketing effectiveness.

Kd.2 Create a system of critical review and appraisal to inform future marketing activity.

Ld.1 Provide professional leadership and develop a cooperative environment to enhance performance.

Ld.2 Promote effective cross-functional working linked to brands and the integration of marketing activities.

Ld.3 Promote and create an environment for career and self-development.

Ld.4 Contribute to organisational change and define and communicate the need for change within the department.

Learning outcomes

Participants will be able to:

- Critically evaluate the techniques available for integrating teams and activities across the organisation, specifically relating to brands and customer-facing processes, and instilling learning within the organisation.

- Identify the barriers to effective implementation of strategies and plans involving change (including communications) in the organisation, and develop measures to prevent or overcome them.

Introduction

- Demonstrate an ability to manage marketing activities as part of strategy implementation.
- Assess an organisation's needs for marketing skills and resources and develop strategies for acquiring, developing and retaining them.
- Initiate and critically evaluate systems for control of marketing activities undertaken as part of business and marketing plans.

Knowledge and skill requirements

Element 1: Creating the organisational context for effective implementation of strategy. (15%)

1.1	Appraise the requirements of a given set of tasks and their context, and assess the impact of relevant factors on the creation or development of a team to perform those tasks.
1.2	Determine the skills, characteristics and roles required within a team to carry out specific tasks effectively.
1.3	Prepare a plan showing how the team should be structures, selected, formed and developed to ensure effective performance.
1.4	Demonstrate an ability to manage the work of teams and individuals to achieve objectives, and create effective working relationships within the team and with other teams.
1.5	Critically evaluate the productivity, satisfaction and effectiveness of teams against their objectives using appropriate techniques.
1.6	Analyse the causes of any sub-optimal performance and recommend how to improve the team's performance, including plans to improve motivation, commitment and loyalty.

Element 2: Managing change and internal marketing. (20%)

2.1	Recommend how an organisation should become more strongly market oriented, taking into account the nature of its environment and culture.
2.2	Assess the main pressures on an organisation to change and the initiatives available or being used to respond.
2.3	Identify and evaluate the sources and the techniques for overcoming any resistance to change.
2.4	Assess the impact of, and prepare a plan for, change in a marketing department, including the development of appropriate skills and capabilities to meet the new objectives.
2.5	Critically evaluate the role and content of an internal marketing communications plan and its contribution to managing change in an organisation.

Element 3: Implementing the business strategy through marketing activities. (30%)

3.1	Explain the link between marketing activities and shareholder value, and measurement using economic value added.
3.2	Determine the contribution to shareholder value of marketing activities undertaken.
3.3	Build sustainability and ethics into business and marketing activities (including the mix) through planning, the instillation of values and day-to-day management.
3.4	Critically appraise methods available for valuing brands and building brand equity, and recommend an appropriate approach for the organisation.
3.5	Propose a contingency plan and procedures to be taken in the event of a 'crisis' or threat to the reputation of the brand or the organisation (including communications with the press and stakeholders).
3.6	Identify 'moments of truth' in delivering a service and activities that may add further value, and assess their likely impact on customers and intermediaries.
3.7	Propose and implement appropriate improvements to customer service by developing or enhancing customer care programmes.
3.8	Establish and apply techniques for managing and monitoring service quality, including the use of specific measures.
3.9	Develop and manage integrated marketing and communications programmes to establish and build relationships appropriate to the needs of customers, clients or intermediaries.
3.10	Develop support for relationships with customers, clients and intermediaries using appropriate information systems and databases and adhering to relevant privacy and data protection legislation.

Element 4: Management techniques for managing the marketing function. (20%)

4.1	Assess the relevance to an organisation of the key concepts of quality management, including structured approaches to continuous improvement and problem solving, and their use in conducting marketing activities.
4.2	Develop a plan for compliance of a marketing function's activities with an organisation's quality management system.
4.3	Assess the relevance to a marketing function of the concept of process and techniques for process management, and develop a plan for their use in conducting marketing activities.
4.4	Assess the relevance to an organisation of the key concepts and techniques of project (or programme) management, and develop plans for their use in conducting marketing and other business activities.
4.5	Assess the capabilities of an organisation to exploit innovation and creativity in its products/services and processes.
4.6	Develop and nurture processes and techniques within marketing teams to exploit innovations in marketing.
4.7	Establish a mechanism, which is consistent with organisational policy, for deciding the activities to be undertaken by external suppliers, including agencies and outsourcing, and gain approval for the relevant expenditure.

Element 5: Measurement, evaluation and control. (15%)

5.1	Develop and use 'accounting' measures of the performance of marketing activities against objectives.
5.2	Define and use customer-related and innovation measures as part of the organisation's balanced scorecard.
5.3	Measure the financial returns achieved on specific investments in marketing activities and programmes and compare them with the original business case or investment appraisal.
5.4	Propose measures of the value generated by developing a position based on sustainability or ethics and of the progress of the organisation in achieving the desired position.
5.5	Assess the value that marketing activities generate and contribute to shareholder value, as appropriate working with colleagues from other disciplines, using appropriate models and techniques.

Assessment

CIM will offer a single form of assessment based on the learning outcomes for this module. It will take the form of an invigilated, time-constrained assessment throughout the delivery network. Candidates' assessments will be marked centrally by CIM.

Overview and rationale

This module is an entirely new departure for CIM, but one which reflects the very real challenges that organisations face in implementing strategy and delivering against plans. As a new syllabus, it is not yet as well served with support materials as other modules, so participants and tutors should be prepared to draw materials from a range of sources.

This module introduces the knowledge and skills required to implement the organisation's strategy by managing its marketing activities. It is important to emphasise that, at this level, we are dealing with business, not purely marketing, decisions. As such, marketing has to integrate with the other functions. This module builds on the Strategic Marketing Decisions module and provides a valuable foundation for the application of implementation knowledge and skills in the final module, Strategic Marketing in Practice. It places a strong emphasis on cross-functional working to integrate teams across the organisation to brand and customer processes.

This module builds on some of the concepts and skills introduced in the Marketing Management in Practice module at Stage 2.

Approach

The challenge in delivering this syllabus is to avoid the pitfall of treating it as a loosely linked set of aspects, each drawn from a different academic discipline. The Statements of Marketing Practice should be used to provide focus on the marketing activities that participants at this level will have to perform in the workplace. The syllabus envisages marketing as either a discrete function or a set of activities spread throughout the organisation. Both of these contexts need to be brought out during delivery.

It is important to emphasise the links between everything the organisation does (its activities), how it does it (people and processes) and why it is doing it (strategic goals, competitive position and customer satisfaction). Success may just be out of reach because of the lack of co-ordination and integration of these important issues. The role of strategic marketing managers, for which this module prepares participants, demands a high level of coordination with colleagues in other disciplines or functions.

Similarly, it is important throughout the delivery of this module to emphasise the marketing and wider organisational context. International marketing strategy is no longer treated as a discrete module but is integrated into all the modules at Stage 3. No organisation is detached from international influences even if the organisation does not have or deal with international customers. Tutors should ensure that they reflect in their delivery approach and materials used the international dimension of implementation.

They should also reflect the different contexts (B2B, B2C, services, capital projects, not-for-profit, voluntary and public sector) in which marketing activities are carried out. A key role of the tutor is to ensure that participants cover a range of contexts and are able to see how marketing may be applied differently. Again this can be achieved through their delivery approach and materials.

Introduction

Syllabus content

Element 1: Creating the organisational context for effective implementation of strategy. (15%)

This element develops an understanding of the formation, development and performance of marketing teams. It draws on the academic theories contained in the academic disciplines of organisational behaviour (OB) and, to a lesser extent, organisational development (OD).

Element 2: Managing change and internal marketing. (20%)

This element provides an understanding of how the strategic marketing manager can influence the organisational culture, in particular into adopting a stronger market orientation. It goes on to address the planning and implementation of change, using the concept of internal marketing, to facilitate and manage the consequent change in the organisation and marketing team. This part of the syllabus draws on the theories of culture and change management.

Element 3: Implementing the business strategy through marketing activities. (30%)

This element covers the strategic marketing manager's role in managing marketing activities within an organisation. It emphasises the link with shareholder value and corporate reputation, reflecting on the increasing importance of sustainability, social responsibility and ethics. It goes on to explore the marketing activities needed to enhance reputation: brand management, service quality and relationships. This part of the syllabus is based on marketing theory but reflects up-to-practice that may not be covered in some marketing texts.

Element 4: Management techniques for managing the marketing function. (20%)

This element aims to equip strategic marketers with some of the key management techniques needed to manage the organisation's marketing activities. It covers concepts and their application drawn from quality, process and project management. It also places importance on instilling creativity and innovation as a means of overcoming obstacles to implementation within organisations. Finally, it touches on the management of external resources and ensuring they contribute to the overall value generated by marketing. The syllabus for this element draws on operations management, including quality management.

Element 5: Measurement, evaluation and control. (15%)

This final element closes the loop in the strategic management process started in the *Analysis & Evaluation* module at Stage 3 by focussing on the measurement of performance and control. It develops an understanding of the various measures and associated techniques available and processes for appraising and evaluating activity, team and business performances. This part of the syllabus draws on financial management and control theory.

Question Bank

Question Bank

1 Participation
40 mins

What are the **disadvantages** of a **participative style** of management? How can these be **minimised?**

(25 marks)

2 Motivation
40 mins

Outline the **principles of motivating employees**. Using illustrations from your own observations, which of these principles seem to you to work in practice, and which do not? Give reasons for each of your answers.

(25 marks)

3 New product development team
40 mins

A colleague has just been appointed as team leader responsible for bringing together a new product development team, drawn from staff across the functional areas of the business. What detailed advice would you give him to ensure this team is able to perform effectively in as short a time as possible?

(25 marks)

4 Planning a team
40 mins

As a **management consultant** you have been approached by the CEO of Xpressions Unlimited to offer advice on planning a team. You are to **write a report** showing how the team should be **selected and developed**, with the addition of a list of **team-building activities**.

(25 marks)

5 Leadership and performance
40 mins

You are the marketing manager for a small printing company and poor leadership in your company has resulted in poor performance and demotivated staff. Prepare a report to your managers outlining how effective leadership can improve individual, team and business performance, particularly from a customer perspective.

(25 marks)

6 Emotional Intelligence (EQ)
40 mins

Current academic argument supports the notion that intellect alone is insufficient as in management many problems encountered are essentially emotional in nature. Goleman suggests a manager's or leader's ability to handle other people's emotions effectively is largely dependent on how they manage their own **emotional state**.

Required

Define **emotional intelligence** and briefly outline why you think there may be a need for it in the workplace today. Suggest also how it can **influence** a manager's skills.

(25 marks)

7 Marketing task
40 mins

As markets fragment and life cycles get shorter and less predictable, the nature of the **marketing task** is changing. **Identify the causes** of these changes and say how a marketing manager can **respond.**

(25 marks)

8 Champion of change
40 mins

The recently appointed Chief Executive Officer (CEO) of PW Storey Ltd is intent on making the organisation more competitive. He has made it clear that costs are too high and productivity too low. The trade union that represents the steel workers in PW Storey Ltd is well organised and has promised the workers that it will defend their wage levels and working conditions.

Required

As the newly appointed **consultant with expertise in managing change**, you have been asked to write a brief report to enlighten the new CEO on the following matters:

(a) State the **forces for change** and likely **causes of resistance** in PW Storey Ltd. Classify these according to whether they can be considered as deriving from **internal or external sources**. (10 marks)

(b) Make recommendations to the newly appointed Chief Executive Officer of PW Storey Ltd and suggest how he might go about managing the process of change. (15 marks)

(25 marks)

9 Marketing orientation
40 mins

Recommend how an organisation can become more **strongly market orientated**. Make particular reference to culture and their environment.

(25 marks)

10 Change and the individual

You are the human resource manager at Mentoes Plc. You have been asked by the managing director to write a report outlining the following;

(a) The **drivers of change** within the organisation (5 marks)
(b) The effect of change on individuals (15 marks)
(c) The **likely barriers** to individual change (5 marks)

(25 marks)

11 Brand stretching

40 mins

As a marketing planner discuss the **key elements of a brand strategy** and the criteria that should be used in brand stretching decisions. Illustrate your answer with examples.

(25 marks)

12 Integrity

40 mins

The discovery of heavily overstated profits in some of the largest US corporations in 2002 undermined investor confidence in company accounts and called into question the integrity of senior managers, their professional staff and the presumed independence of external auditors.

Required

(a) Describe the **key influences** on the **ethical conduct** of senior management of business corporations, their professional staff and those involved with auditing their accounts.

(12 marks)

(b) Explain what both businesses and professional bodies can do to **influence ethical behaviour** of their organisational members. (13 marks)

(25 marks)

13 Hotel Company

40 mins

You have applied for a job with a small hotel company that is establishing a **formal marketing function** for the first time. As part of the interview process, you have been asked to make a **short presentation** that explains **the characteristics of marketing in the service sector**. Prepare some notes covering the areas you intend to deal with in your presentation.

(25 marks)

14 Crisis Management

40 mins

Since 'September 11th', crisis management has become a significant issue for all organisations. In light of this, organisations have been made aware of the need to have a contingency plan and procedures in place in the event of a threat to their reputation.

Required

As the newly appointed **public relations officer** with Jarrod & Jarrod Inc., you have been asked to prepare a report for the Board of Directors, outlining a **contingency plan and procedures** to be taken in the event of a crisis.

(25 marks)

15 Relationship marketing and IT technology

40 mins

Define **relationship marketing** and show how **IT technology** can help develop and **support relationships** with customers, employees and suppliers.

(25 marks)

16 Measuring the value of brands
40 mins

You have recently been appointed as brand manager for Springbok Foods. With the knowledge that that **brand creation** is very expensive, you have been asked to submit a report to the Board of Directors, offering advice on how the organisation can **value their brand**.

(25 marks)

17 Shareholder value analysis
40 mins

Marketing has always suffered from a lack of **true business value**. Show how **shareholder value analysis** can assist in overcoming this.

(25 marks)

18 Brand strategies and equity
40 mins

As a newly appointed brand manager, you have been asked by the marketing director to prepare a report outlining and evaluating various **branding strategies.** You have also been asked to outline the principles **of brand equity.**

(25 marks)

19 Ethics and social responsibility
40 mins

In the 21st Century, business is faced with the knowledge that there has been a rise in the **'ethical consumer'**. As the **ethical consultant** employed by Watson & Flounders, an old established family business, you have been asked to bring them up-to-date with current thinking and advise on how to **build ethics into the business and marketing activities**. Illustrate your answer with examples.

(25 marks)

20 Service quality
40 mins

As the newly appointed **customer relations manager**, you have been requested by the CEO of Realto Hotels to prepare a report demonstrating the importance of **service quality** and to outline a **customer care programme** for the organisation.

(25 marks)

21 Push and pull
40 mins

An office furniture manufacturing company is about to launch a new range of products.

(a) Explain what is meant by a push communication strategy and contrast this with a pull communication strategy. (13 marks)

(b) Briefly outline the main characteristics of the marketing communications mix used to reach members of the marketing channel. (12 marks)

(25 marks)

22 RUS plc 40 mins

Jacaranda plc operates a chain of hotels. Its strategy has been to provide medium-priced accommodation for business people during the week and for families at weekends. The market has become increasingly competitive and they have decided to change their strategy. In future, they will provide 'a high-quality service for the discerning guest'.

Required

(a) Explain the relevance of a programme of **'total quality management'** for Jacaranda plc in the implementation of its new strategy. (13 marks)

(b) Summarise the financial and organisational implications of Jacaranda plc's new strategy. (12 marks)

(25 marks)

23 Great Utility Services Ltd 40 mins

Great Utility Services Ltd (GUSL), has been formed by centralising a number of regional management units in the holding company, Great Utility. GUSL, which provides a variety of technical services, has been formed so that Great Utility will benefit from economies of scale. GUSL will sell its services to other companies in the water industry and other industries e.g. brewing, chemicals and public sector organisations such as hospitals. Water firms need to introduce metering technology so that water can be priced according to usage. User firms are seeking to manage their use of water more effectively as part of their contribution to environmental concerns, and GUSL is there to help them.

A major issue to be facing GUSL relates to information associated with the introduction of metering technology. A strategy needs to be introduced for the management of the information and a new system needs to be installed. Attention to the accounting system is felt to be most urgent. Senior management has stipulated project management techniques are to be used in introducing the new systems.

Required - As **project manager**, you have been asked by GUSL to outline the following:

(a) What are the **distinguishing characteristics of project management** and how can its success be defined? (7 marks)

(b) Describe the **project management techniques** that can be used to introduce new information systems to GUSL, and to minimise the risk of the project failing **to meet its objectives** (9 marks)

(c) Outline the **skills and attributes** of a good project manager. (9 marks)

(25 marks)

24 Project guide to conferences 40 mins

Your Company is about to launch a new product in hand-held digital technology. You have been asked to prepare a **project guide to planning** the launch at Expo International Centre. Included in the plan you should highlight the actions to be taken before, during and after the sales launch.

(25 marks)

25 Creativity and Innovation

40 mins

Doogle and McHeggarty Ltd are a small but growing organisation. Following the loss of a major account, it has been identified that there is need to develop a culture that encourages individuals to question what they do, how they do it, explore new horizons and exploit new opportunities to ensure the organisation is proactive in realising changes in customer needs.

Required

As **the Human Resource Consultant** brought in to oversee the necessary changes, you are to prepare a report outlining the conditions required to:

1. Foster **creativity and innovation** in individuals in the organisation.
2. **Nurture the processes** that support the development of creativity in all areas within the organisation.

(25 marks)

26 Creative people

40 mins

As a result of the competitive global developments leading to increasing marginality, new markets have to be continuously sought and created. Today customers are faced with more choice and their requirements are constantly changing. Reaction to this has been that product standards and technology are continuously improving. Therefore, to keep abreast of consumer needs and wants and maintain a profitable market share, the communications message for a product or service has to be creative to stand out from the pack.

Required

Outline **the characteristics** that make up **creative people** who are likely to stand out from the rest and suggest how these characteristics can be nurtured within a marketing team and how the characteristics can be applied in the business context. Illustrate your answer with **relevant examples**.

(25 marks)

27 Outsourcing marketing activity

40 mins

You are a Marketing Manager in the textile industry and your organisation (with a strong brand) intends to outsource many functions. You have been asked:

(a) How you will identify the marketing skills required over the next three years
(b) Reasons for and against marketing activities being outsourced
(c) For your ideas on what could be outsourced and what should remain in-house

(25 marks)

28 Innovation

40 mins

Innovation is often referred to as the **'life blood'** of an organisation. Evaluate this statement, identify the **potential barriers to innovation**, and discuss the means by which organisations can improve their ability to innovate. Use examples to illustrate your answer.

(25 marks)

Question Bank

29 Planning for growth *40 mins*

You work for a software company and your Managing Director has announced plans to grow the business by 35% in the next two years. The product range will be extended to support this growth. Write a report to the Managing Director on the Human Resource planning issues involved and how you intend to identify and ensure appropriate marketing skills levels to support this growth.

(25 marks)

30 Managing outside suppliers

You have been asked to write an article for *Marketing Business* which describes the types of outside resources which various Marketing Directors use, that suggests how outside suppliers should be briefed, and indicates how the relationship with such suppliers might be managed and controlled. You should use examples throughout the article to illustrate the points you raise.

(25 marks)

31 Relationship marketing *40 mins*

As the relationship marketing manager at an airline of your choice, you have been given the task of identifying which aspects of the extended relationship marketing mix may be particularly effective in maintaining high customer retention rates for the company. In a report to the marketing director, illustrate how each element of the mix may be relevant to your airline in its efforts to keep its customers.

(20 marks)

32 Quality management *40 mins*

As the newly appointed Quality Assurance Manager at Blouberg Electronic Industries, you have been asked by the CEO to provide an **outline of methods of quality control, assurance and improvement**.

(25 marks)

33 Expenditure *40 mins*

As a **marketing manager** write a short article for inclusion in a company magazine suggesting how the amount of money spent on **marketing communications might be strategically important**. Use examples to illustrate your article.

(25 marks)

34 Feedback and control system *40 mins*

What **factors** should be taken into account in the **development of a marketing feedback and control system?** In what ways might the information possibly be used?

(25 marks)

35 Balanced scorecard
40 mins

From a marketing point of view, show how the **balanced scorecard** can be used as a technique to **evaluate business performance**.

(25 marks)

36 Budgeting
40 mins

Budgeting is the most common **control mechanism**. Outline the factors influencing the budget and the problems encountered in setting one. Also, tabulate the different methods for **setting a marketing budget** and make comments on each.

(25 marks)

37 Royal Shakespeare Company
80 mins

The employees and the brand –
The importance of communications and motivation

Reform in the arts has not experienced the same management revolution as, for example, the health service or public utilities. In the world of entertainment, particularly the theatre, the role of management is often misunderstood and undervalued. The Royal Shakespeare Company (RSC) is a company well known for its performances in the theatre. It has now experienced a management revolution that has transformed the way it works. This is to ensure it delivers the highest standards of quality, maximises accessibility to the public and adds value to the lives of those who come into contact with the company.

The RSC has its own special problems, including pay that cannot compete with commercial theatre or television and the 18 month contract periods that deter many big screen actors who need to be able to undertake filming assignments at relatively short notice.

To overcome these problems new contracts have been written to allow more flexibility and increased training and development opportunities have added value to the time people spend with the company. The new approach is reaping its rewards with major British actors reappearing with RSC, some after a 20 year absence. A shorter London season and more resources put into regional partnerships and tours has ensured that 80% of the UK's population now live within an hour's drive of an RSC production.

While those that provide funds and many other external stakeholders have welcomed the changes, media interviews with RSC actors uncovered uncertainties about the RSC's vision and reasons behind the changes.

Staff surveys were conducted and it emerged that too little consultation had taken place with the actors before the changes were implemented. Internal communications are to blame and management agreed that an objective analysis was needed.

Findings from the staff surveys revealed actors' perceptions of the company were confused. For example, management and the board were seen to be elusive and their role was not understood.

It raised the question of how to create effective communications between managers and actors and how to communicate the corporate goals beyond those of making a success of each RSC production. Management specifically wanted to know why artists want to work with RSC and how they could make the company as attractive as possible to them. It also emerged that few actors who jointed RSC realised what to expect. Rehearsal schedules are demanding – 10.00 am to 5.00 pm – followed by an evening performance (6 each week plus 2 matinees). Actors can be performing in up to three different productions simultaneously. Touring makes different demands with actors living in temporary accommodation from week to week, enduring months away from their families. This also makes them feel remote from the rest of the organisation.

There is recognition by management that the RSC band is crucial to success and that the brand is the people involved with the company, particularly actors.

Adapted from an article in People Management

You are the newly appointed marketing manager and the Board have requested that you prepare a report that makes recommendations on the following:

(a) How you would undertake an **audit of current internal communication activities**. Include all forms of communications, for example written, management style and interpersonal skills. (15 marks)

(b) The **design of an induction programme** that will improve the perceptions and expectations of newly recruited actors of the RSC. (10 marks)

(c) How you would **develop and implement an internal communications plan** that improves the process of communications, motivation and team spirit. Briefly explain how this would contribute towards improving the RSC brand. (25 marks)

(50 marks)

38 International Sonatas Hotels

80 mins

The International Sonatas Group has been developing over the last ten years. By a series of new developments and acquisitions the group now owns over 50 hotels in capital cities and international business centres around the world.

The Central Marketing and Business Development Department are responsible for strategy, policy (eg house style for advertisements) and international marketing communications. This includes an excellent interactive website, which gives full details of the hotels around the world and provides online booking facilities.

'City Sonata'

A spirit of revival had spread over the new development area. Twenty years ago this was a wasteland of industrial decay, now there were modern office buildings housing major international organisations, with more major projects under construction. With good road and rail links and easy access to the international airport the area is perfect for international business operations.

'City Sonata' is nearing its final phase, with completion only a few months away. A totally modern hotel with full conference facilities, it had been built to the highest standards of comfort, with every facility for the business traveller. For leisure activities, the hotel is located a few minutes from the romantic waterside. The city centre arts area (which has a full range of attractions: theatres, concert halls, museums, art galleries, etc) is only a short rail or taxi ride away.

'City Sonata' is the group's first development in this country, but it is intended to be a 'flagship' venture, with plans for several other hotels located at other major commercial centres around the country.

Your role

You are Sam Smith and you have just been appointed as marketing manager for 'City Sonata'. You are to be responsible for the development of a small marketing team to market 'City Sonata' within the framework set by the corporate marketing function.

The opening date is in six months' time.

Note. In the above context 'City Sonata' can be considered to be located in any international commercial city of your choice.

Questions for this case study are as follows:

(a) You have to **recruit and build** your own small **marketing team** with the assistance of the local human resource manager. How would you go about **selecting, training, building and motivating** your marketing team? (30 marks)

(b) Part of the role is 'to assist management in the development of a marketing customer care orientation for all staff in the hotel'.

    (i) What **internal marketing activities** would you consider appropriate to developing a **customer care culture** for all the hotel staff? (10 marks)

    (ii) How would you **monitor** the level of client-perceived **service quality**? (10 marks)

(50 marks)

39 Family doctor

80 mins

Conversations with a family doctors' general practice manager

'They felt threatened, I suppose. That's why I was appointed. After years of security and growth the ground had shifted beneath them. Hard work was no longer enough to ensure success. Legislation which created the General Practitioner's Contract of 1990, for example, had reduced the level of capitation fees (and the proportion of a General Practitioner's salary which they represented). At the same time it introduced a payment by results system whereby General Practitioners had to earn additional revenue through attaining target outcomes in problem areas such as cervical smears, childhood immunisation and periodic health checks. Clearly, it was going to pay to be even more customer orientated, and we have a range of customers.

The doctors who are partners in the practice had responded to this new tighter control by the Department of Health through a series of *ad hoc* initiatives designed to protect and grow their business. The partners had found it difficult, initially, to think about their practice in terms of being a business. I think they realised, however, that a new situation, calling for new project developments and a new professional managerial approach on top of their traditional and heavy workloads, required the introduction of some professional help. That is where I came in.

Their largely unconsidered decisions about the changes they should make to the practice had created some new problems. For example, the support staff were demotivated. They felt as though they were being asked to do a lot of new jobs for the sole benefit of the partners. A 'them and us' atmosphere prevailed. Some of them, I am sure, were passively working against the successful implementation of the new ideas. I have had to work on this problem.

I have also had problems related to the power nuances of the practice. For example, I do not have much power with which to impose my preferred ways of changing the enterprise. Rather, I have to undertake reasoned persuasion. It doesn't always work and I do not always get my own way. Another power problem involved one of the clerical administrators whose position as the sole expert on our computer system meant that we were too dependent on him.

Also, I have problems because the partners do not share a common vision for the organisation. One of them is ready for retirement and not so interested in the longer term viability of the group. Another, I think, sees this practice as a career stepping stone. The other two, however, are more interested in the longer-term success of the practice and I was gratified, recently, to hear one of them talk about the need for us to agree a vision for the practice. He also raised the idea of us going off for a half-day, or so, to undertake some sort of brain-storming session for our future.

Another big problem is information, or to put it more accurately, our lack of it. For example, we have no means for ensuring the success of anti-smoking measures. We don't even know how many of our patients smoke. Neither did anybody realise, until after I'd done some investigations, that the partners' gentlemanly approach to the development of the patient list wasn't being reciprocated by all of our neighbourhood practice colleagues. One of the bigger practices nearby has been actively recruiting our patients.

We do have a number of strengths, however. I do think we have a good reputation as a family practice and our range and locations of health promotion clinics is good. The practice is also learning to learn from initiatives being taken in other areas and is prepared to try out new ideas for the benefit of our clients. A recently introduced Exercise Clinic is one example of the sorts of change taking place in the practice.

Also, unlike many of our competitors we are taking full part in the strategic activity of our Health Authority which, as you know, is an important resources supplier to organisations such as ours. One of our partners is a member of the Authority's Family Health Committee. This keeps us close to an important aspect of our environment and helps to protect us from surprises. Currently we are monitoring developments in the moves to take selected secondary health care activities out of the hospital consultancy services.

Obviously, we need to build on our strengths and develop our weaker points. All in all, this is an exciting and challenging job. I am glad they offered it to me and I am glad that I accepted the post.'

Required

(a) Using appropriate analytical techniques, identify and evaluate the key internal and external issues facing the doctors' practice described above. (25 marks)

(b) Advise the new practice manager in her role as an agent of organisational change. Discuss some of the problems she is already facing or is likely to face in her attempts to introduce a more professional approach to the management of the practice and offer advice on how she might address these problems. (25 marks)

(50 marks)

40 Silvadawn Leisurewear   80 mins

The company Silvadawn Leisurewear declares it is a 'high quality leisure wear manufacturing retailer'. Founded by Jessica Silva in the UK in 1976 it prides itself by sourcing materials locally. They have achieved unprecedented success with over 160 branches. As a result of continued growth, by the late 1980s the company had international ambitions and opened branches in Spain, Portugal, Belgium and Holland. In 2004 there is also a substantial mail order business that sells through a widely distributed catalogue and over the Internet.

Retail Stores

The 'High Street' retail side of the business thrived in the 1990s as more and more people started to address their work life balance and sought leisure activity. The company diversified beyond clothing into activity based equipment ie bicycles and outdoor sports equipment. These new product lines brought increasing demands for specialist knowledge amongst the staff, and a systematic effort was made to recruit appropriate individuals from either a hobby/interest background or from competitor organisations. However, recently there has been an increasing feeling in the company that the diversified product range was proving to be unsustainable in the retail operation.

The Mail Order Operation

Silvadawn Leisurewear prides itself on good customer service and believes that this is they way to forge ahead. However, recently staff consultative meetings at the Call Centre have revealed worrying signs. Team leaders have reported that some staff have been making promises to customers about delivery dates which simply cannot be met and customers have been promised refunds even on items which they have worn. There is also an overall concern that some staff respond inconsistently with customers.

A recent review by an external consultant has identified the following issues:

- Sales have decreased and customer complaints have increased on the original product lines of leisurewear.

- High staff turnover amongst specialist staff in retail branches has often left branch managers without appropriate product knowledge to handle detailed customer enquiries.

- Fierce competition in the specialist areas of bicycles and outdoor sports equipment from specialist retailers. Competitors are gaining cost advantage through selling imported goods.

- Personnel inefficiencies are increasing and the cost of running the Call Centre is proving to be expensive.

Following receipt of the report, it was decided to make a major strategic shift in the organisation and focus on a 'New Vision for the 21st Century'. This includes plans to:

- Return to the 'core business' of manufacturing and retailing leisurewear only.

- Restrict the sale of bicycles and outdoor sports equipment to the Internet and mail order operations only.

- Re-focus on quality service.

- Revisit the resource purchasing policy and source some of the clothing from manufacturing operations in China.

- Review the call centre operations for mail order with a view to re-directing operations to India.

Note: The above case is based on a fictitious company for assessment purposes.

Required

(a) What are the **implications** for Silvadawn Leisurewear in **outsourcing** some of the clothing from China? (25 marks)

(b) What are the **advantages and disadvantages** of re-directing the Call Centre to India? (25 marks)

(50 marks)

41 CiniCentre 80 mins

The CiniCentre was established in 1960 as a charitable trust to promote and increase public awareness of the cinema as an entertainment and cultural medium. The CiniCentre is managed through a part-time board of governors drawn from representatives of the film industry, from government nominees and from elected nominees of the membership of the CiniCentre Film Institute. The board of governors delegate executive responsibility to a chief executive officer (CEO). CiniCentre has five major activity areas or operational divisions each of which has its own manager. These are as follows.

- The multi-screen Film Theatre (FT) which provides performances for the general public of new releases, classic films and minority interest films.

- The Museum of the Cinema (MoC) which provides a permanent exhibition of the history and development of the film industry.

- The Globe restaurant, bars and cafeteria, which are open to cinema goers and to the general public.

- The Film Archive Unit (FAU), which is concerned with the transfer of old film archive material to video as a means of long-term preservation.

- The CiniCentre Film Institute (CFI), membership of which is open to members of the public by annual subscription. Members receive preferential bookings to events, seat discounts and a free copy of CiniCentre's monthly magazine, 'Film Fan'. The magazine and associated publishing activities also form part of the responsibilities of the film institute.

In addition to the five business units there are also three support units which provide common support services as follows.

- Administration - office services, finance, personnel, computing
- Buildings - building maintenance, cleaning, security, repairs and renewals
- Maintenance - technical and technician support for the repair and maintenance of capital equipment

The three support units come under the control of a Head of Support Services.

The CiniCentre is partly funded by government grant and partly funded from its own commercial activities. However, as a part of government policy to reduce the contribution to the arts, the grant to the CiniCentre will, over the next three years, be reduced by 20%. A financial summary of the current year's operations of the CiniCentre is provided in Table 1.

John Umbasa has recently taken over as chief executive officer of CiniCentre. He has been recruited from a senior position in an international media business. The board of governors at CiniCentre were directed by the government to bring in an external CEO as a result of a series of management problems, which have attracted considerable adverse publicity. These have included the following.

- A failure to stay within government financial guidelines of not operating an annual financial deficit.
- Press criticism about the loss of archive film due to the failure to speed up the transfer to video tape.
- Further press criticism on the recent imposition of an admission charge to the Museum of the Cinema.
- Reports of poor quality service and expensive food in the Globe restaurants.
- Persistent labour relations problems with the public sector staff trade union, which represents almost all the non-managerial museum, film theatre, clerical and catering staff.
- Complaints from the CFI membership that the film season has concentrated too much on popular income earning mainstream films with a subsequent fall in the number of showings of classic and non-English language films.

John Umbasa realises that he faces major challenges in revitalising the CiniCentre organisation and dealing with the proposed sharp reduction in government funding. He believes that what the CiniCentre needs is a vision of its role and priorities plus management control systems which link performance to clear-cut divisional objectives. He has offered you a one year management consultancy contract to assist him.

Table 1 - summary financial data

All figures in £m	Commercial income	Direct costs	Apportioned indirect costs	Surplus/(deficit)
Film Theatre	1.20	1.70	0.86	(1.36)
Museum	0.25	2.20	1.11	(3.06)
Globe Catering	1.70	0.90	0.45	0.35
Film Archive	0.00	3.20	1.62	(4.82)
CFI	2.30	1.90	0.96	(0.56)
Total	5.45	9.90	5.00	(9.45)
Government grant				9.00
Surplus/(deficit)				(0.45)

Required

The CiniCentre Charitable Trust has been directed by the Government to address a series of management problems. John Umbasa has been hired as the new CEO to address the matter. His background is in private enterprise where profit is the bottom line. He has identified that there is no clear vision of the organisation or any evidence of formalised process for strategic planning. He has therefore decided to undertake an analysis starting with the internal and external stakeholder groups.

Explain how:

(a) (i) **Stakeholder analysis** can assist John with formulating the organisation's vision, objectives and goals.

(ii) Identify four different Cinicentre stakeholder groups **indicating** their **potential power, influence** and **likely expectations**. (25 marks)

(b) Prepare a short management **briefing paper** for presentation to the next meeting of the Board of Governors outlining a more formalised **strategic management process**.

(20 marks)

(c) At present management control is based purely on **budgetary conditions**. Briefly outline another **performance measurement indicator** (PMI) that is not purely financial and can be used as a means of **strategic control**. (5 marks)

(50 marks)

42 Paperworks plc

80 mins

Paperworks plc is the leading supplier of coloured and specialist paper in Europe producing paper for a number of different market sectors. They operate in over 50 countries on five continents. Turnover in 2002 was £54 million with a profit of £4 million. The company was founded over 150 years ago and continues to be a family run business employing approximately 500 staff.

The organisation has recently fought off the threat of a take-over by a multinational paper making company and is committed to remaining an independent company. However, this threat has prompted the senior management team to undertake a detailed review of their current position and strategic direction.

A key factor contribution to the success of the company lies in their ability to produce high quality papers consistently, that are tailored to meet individual customer requirements. Ongoing research programmes ensure that the company remains at the cutting edge of paper technology. However, this is often not linked to market needs. Paperworks has flexible production planning that ensures they can deal with large orders as well as short runs. A further factor contributing to the success of the company lies in their relationship with their agents in international markets. The company has worked hard to develop these relationships through a team of export managers that travel regularly to ensure the agents are well supported and continue to be committed to purchasing from Paperworks.

The paper and boards industry consists of six major sectors: newsprint, printing and writing paper, corrugated card materials, soft tissues, board and packaging papers. Paperworks operates mainly in two markets: packaging and printing and writing paper. Within these they have identified a number of niche markets such as luxury packaging, brochures, framing, bookbinding and archiving materials. These prove to be profitable markets but many are very specialised. The marketing director is keen to continue to grow the number of niche markets they operate in, but at the same time wishes to increase sales in more volume related products such as greetings cards. Paperworks competes with a range of competitors depending on the market sector. Table 1 identifies the current markets in which they operate along with selected market and competitor data for 2002.

Table 1. Selected market and competitor data for 2002

Market Sector	Paperwork plc Sales (£m)	Number of Companies competing in Market Sector	Sales of 3 largest companies (£m)			Forecast Market Sector Growth Rate (%)
Bookbinding papers	8	4	*8	4	4	0
Packaging	12	10	*12	12	5	16
Magazines	6	8	18	17	15	4
Business Stationery	15	12	*5	10	9	8
Photographic paper	8	5	10	*8	7	12
Greetings cards	5	15	25	22	17	2
Total	54					

* Denotes Paperworks' sales within the sector.

Source: Fictitious data prepared for case study purposes only.

Customers include general printers, publishers of periodicals and books and manufacturers and retailers of well-known branded products such as Rolex, Christian Dior, Chanel and Marks & Spencer. The latter are purchasing luxury packaging to improve the image of their international brands.

Despite the many strengths of the company an internal review has highlighted a number of weaknesses such as slow response to environmental changes, a costly distribution system (they currently maintain their own fleet of vehicles) and an ineffective website that is currently little more than an online brochure. The majority of sales and profit come from products that were developed over five years ago.

Demand for paper follows fairly closely to the rate of general economic activity and in the last 10 years consumption has nearly doubled. The pattern of paper usage in industry and commerce is likely to change due to the growth of interactive electronic media. However, consumption is still forecast to grow over the next 10 years. The papermaking sector consists of a range of different markets, many of which are mature whilst others are at growth stage. The sector is subject to a number of pressures.

There is a continuing pressure in terms of the environment, made worse by Paperworks' location in a Site of Special Scientific Interest (SSSI), cost of raw materials, cost of distribution, and the continuing threat of terrorism that has had a major impact on travel and tourism, which are some of the company's key markets.

In particular there is a threat from a key competitor, Universal Paper, which is challenging them in a number of key markets, where they are currently market leaders. Universal Paper's operations are located in South America where there is easy access to raw materials and cheap labour. This is enabling them to operate at low cost and undercut Paperworks' prices. Universal Paper is dealing with direct sales and has developed a highly sophisticated website that enables customers to request samples, view current samples and place and track orders.

In the past 20 years recycled material has become important in the production of low-grade forms of paper such as newsprint. Paperworks realises that some of its customers are seeking high quality products made from recycled products and sees this as an opportunity. They are currently in discussions with a company that makes high-grade pulp from recycled paper to explore the opportunity of establishing a strategic alliance.

Note: The above case is based on a fictitious company for assessment purposes.

Required

(a) The managing director is concerned that the organisation is not sufficiently innovative. You have been asked to **identify the reasons** why this may be the case and to **provide recommendations** as to how the company can **increase** the **pace of innovation** within the company. (25 marks)

(b) As highlighted in the recent company internal review, the **website** has been deemed **ineffective**.

    (i) How can Paperworks improve their online capability? (10 marks)

    (ii) What **measures** can they use for **monitoring effectiveness** on the internet? (10 marks)

    (iii) Outline the **Privacy and Data Protection** regulation and legislation. (5 marks)

(50 marks)

43 Selfridges

80 mins

Founded by Gordon Selfridge in 1858 with the vision that shopping should be seen as entertainment and fun, by the 1990s the Selfridges brand was in decline. Their story is one of reinvention and growth in which people management has played a vital role in creating what is now a highly successful retail chain. In 1965 the Sears retailing empire took control. Over the years it could not attract top brands and Sears were resisting spending money on it. It was seen as the poor relation to Harrods and department stores were generally thought of as dinosaurs of the retail industry. In early 1992 some refurbishment was carried out which was deemed so successful in terms of increased sales that a master plan for refurbishing the whole of the store was devised. In 1997 a de-merger was announced and the store returned to its original name of Selfridges & Co.

What was once a 'fusty' old department store began its renewal process in the mid-1990s with the appointment of a new senior management team and in 1996 a new CEO who believed that unless changes were made, Selfridges would eventually close and die. His stated aim was to become 'a store for the next century'. Selfridges now markets itself as the 'House of Brands' with its own strong image based on that assumption.

The organisational structure where head office functions were subsumed in the retail function making it difficult to see where responsibilities lay was changed in 2001 to a multi-site retail format. Five functional directors now report to the CEO. Each functional director has his or her own staff of senior managers. Business managers (one each for menswear, womenswear, home and cosmetics) report to each of the general managers of the store. Business managers, in turn, are responsible for sales managers, each of whom is responsible for one or more departments.

In transforming its employment culture to complement the change, Selfridges adopted a series of initiatives. It conducted culture surveys, organised focus groups and replaced its old job evaluation scheme with a broadbanding pay arrangement. Great emphasis has been put on training and development with the aim to make it fun as well as useful. There is now an emphasis on a coaching approach to help staff learn from their own experiences in contrast to traditional teaching and training. The directors sponsor the management development programmes and managers, in turn, learn how to develop their staff.

Selfridges have made the explicit effort to model the underlying stakeholder values required in its dealings with customers, employees, the local community, suppliers and other stakeholders.

These values are expressed under four goals to be 'aspirational, friendly, accessible and bold'. For each goal it asked the following questions:

- Employee values: how does this make me want to work here?
- Customer values: how am I encouraged to shop here?
- Community values: how does Selfridges reflect the spirit of the city?
- Shareholder values: why should I invest in the store?
- Supplier values: what makes Selfridges an interesting proposition?

The table below gives an example of how these questions, under the 'friendly' heading, are answered.

THE VALUES MATRIX: 'FRIENDLY'				
Employee Values *How does this make me want to work here?*	**Customer Values** *How am I encouraged to shop here?*	**Community Values** *How does Selfridges reflect the spirit of the city?*	**Shareholder Values** *Why should I invest in the store?*	**Supplier Values** *What makes Selfridges an interesting proposition?*
Selfridges is a friendly place to work. I like my manager and my team.	People at Selfridges are always smiling and helpful. They seem to enjoy working there.	Selfridges promotes an inclusive spirit.	The annual reports are inviting and easy to read.	We help each other in the continuous improvement of our relationship.
I know that my opinion and contribution are welcomed.	I like to buy and browse in Selfridges. I never feel under pressure, but rarely come home empty-handed.	Selfridges is a microcosm of all the different communities that make up the city life.	The financial information is transparent and the Directors are open to any questions.	The diverse range of high-quality products adds value to my product.
I feel welcomed and this makes me welcome others.	Selfridges represents the good things about city living.	Through its managers and staff, Selfridges gets involved in community projects.	I feel welcome whenever I attend shareholder meetings.	My concession staff are treated well and made to feel welcome.

Note: The 'friendly' section of the matrix describes how this value should affect all stakeholders.

This matrix of values contains bold statements and the company have faced many challenges making them work. For example, when launching the new Manchester store in 1998 the traditional working patterns in the area were broken. Staff had to be found for long opening hours and for weekends and evenings, with key people working to a rota. Public transport was poor, especially at the end of the evening shift, which made recruitment and retention harder. Staff turnover, particularly in the first few years, was high – although not bad compared with the retail industry as a whole – but the company did cut it from 78 % in 2000 to 40% in 2001.

Of course, nothing is perfect: one of the problems with value statements is that they raise expectations. A survey of the staff in the first year revealed that 46% of respondents said they wanted more recognition and appreciation, two-thirds said they were hardly ever asked by managers for their views. One interviewee put it: 'Managers should have a more relaxed, approachable attitude. They should ask staff what problems they have and be more involved on the shop floor'.

The staff who were satisfied with their manager's behaviour had positive attitudes towards their employer and were happy with their jobs, career opportunities and the appraisal system. But according to the respondents, not enough managers were performing to the level they expected. Selfridges took this on board and asked the team leaders to reapply for their own jobs, which led to departures in some cases.

A survey conducted in the second year revealed that staff duly found improvements. For example, they perceived a significant increase in the amount of respect they received from line managers and there was a much wider belief that managers were good at responding to their suggestions. The proportion of staff that were satisfied with the appraisal system rose from 59% to 84%. One interviewee said: 'We have a manager who gets the appraisal done. We receive praise now and even little gifts such as perfume'.

During the survey, staff at Selfridges displayed one of the highest levels of commitment out of the 12 organisations researched. The factors they particularly linked to job satisfaction, motivation and commitment were challenging work; job security; teamwork; career opportunities; appraisal; and most of all communication, involvement and the way their managers managed.

In the period at the end of the 2-year survey, sales were up 23% on the previous year, payroll costs were down 5%, while 'contribution' – the key measure of sales against payroll costs – had increased by 32%. Selfridges now has a raft of performance measures covering staff satisfaction, productivity and customer satisfaction (measured through the use of mystery shoppers).

Adapted from People Management 2003

Required

(a) Outline how effective leadership has transformed Selfridges and discuss what qualities are needed for the leader in the 21st Century. Illustrate with relevant examples. (25 marks)

(b) What are the internal and external factors affecting the organisation? (25 marks)

(50 marks)

44 Woodstock Furniture

80 mins

Woodstock Furniture is a privately owned company located in a fashionable area in London. The company makes bespoke, high quality kitchen and bathroom furniture. Kitchens account for 80% of sales and the average order value is £25,000.

The general kitchen furniture market in the UK is worth over £800 million but of this the bespoke market is only worth a static 1%. Woodstock's sales have fluctuated over its 22 years of trading and currently stand at £1.7 million per annum with net profit at 6.9%. However, the balance sheet is weak and there is little opportunity to attract finance for promotional investment. Staff are very supportive of the company, appear to identify strongly with the customised approach and many have been with the company since its start up. However, many of the internal systems and procedures are old, slow and in need of updating - perhaps a reflection of the slower, detailed craftsmanlike culture that identifies the Woodstock Furniture Company.

In recognition of some of the problems facing the company, the management has developed a marketing plan which seeks growth of 15% per annum to be achieved by market penetration and in particular, the attraction of new customers. It now needs a marketing communication programme to develop a strong corporate brand. The problem is that profit margins are small and there is little to invest in developing the brand and competing with well known high street outlets.

The competition, as Woodstock see it, have huge resources which can be used to invest in promotional campaigns to drive awareness and action. For example, these companies have authentic web sites, unlike Woodstock's site which is little more than an online brochure. Many of the large national standardised companies can produce promotional literature in large production runs and are happy to ignore wastage. Using expert photography of 'pretend' kitchens, the quality and impact of the literature is high. Woodstock's smaller budgets dictate that photographs of real customers' kitchens are required, which seldom look perfect and can even appear amateurish. It costs £4 to produce each of the Woodstock brochures so vetting of each request for literature is important to avoid those people who ask for brochures but buy nothing. A high conversion rate is necessary and although 50% of quotations are converted into sales, Woodstock cannot afford this figure to be lowered.

Woodstock's customers do not want the standardised kitchen units provided by the larger, more dominant players in the market They want kitchens made to measure and which complement the character of their homes. They look for attention to detail, design, craftsmanship and support when commissioning bespoke companies such as Woodstock. The target market is affluent, often has more than one home and relies on word of mouth recommendation when drawing up a shortlist of possible providers. For many, price is not the key issue - rather it is the capability to craft suitable furniture to match the required decor and house style. This requires a high degree of trust, which successful companies in this market are able to reciprocate and in turn generate commitment. Many of Woodstock's customers are celebrities but because discretion and privacy is important to them, they often refuse to allow their names (and kitchens) to be used for Woodstock publicity. However, customer loyalty is extremely important with over 60% of new business being driven from existing customers.

In recognition of this, Woodstock now believes that it is in the business of craftsmanship and the design and construction of customised furniture rather than the business of making and installing kitchen and bathroom furniture. It has improved levels of support and service (having, for example, introduced annual maintenance contracts) and has high levels of customer satisfaction. The marketing plan states that prices are to be raised to capitalise on premium pricing opportunities and the high levels of demand inelasticity. The marketing plan involves forming relationships with architects and developers and creating cross promotions and alliances with firms operating in similar markets, such as conservatories, studies and staircases.

Source: Adapted from an article in the Sunday Times, 15 August 1999.

Required

As a marketing adviser you have been asked to help the company achieve its objectives. In particular you are to prepare an Integrated Marketing Communications Plan for Woodstock Furniture covering the next two years. It is important to justify your recommendations and state any assumptions made in order to prepare the plan. **(50 marks)**

45 Campaigns of global pressure 80 mins

It has been suggested that big business has more to fear from the activities of Corporate Social Responsibility (CSR) – pressure groups such as Greenpeace, Amnesty International and Global Exchange than it has from the activities of Trade Unions. These groups have long been influential on issues such as the environment, marketing standards, public safety, financial propriety and animal rights. They are also increasingly effective in areas that were once the domain of the Trade Unions (TU). A number of companies eg Shell (Brent Spar), Nestlé (baby milk powder) Union Carbide (Bhopal), Perrier (benzine) and Enron etc. can testify to the effectiveness of their campaigns.

Rightly or wrongly, many people already associate certain multi-national businesses with child labour or the operation of global sweatshops. We have recently seen many references in the media to 'fat cat pay' and severance packages in major companies. It is not the TU that have brought these stories to the media's attention but organisations such as Oxfam, Anti-Slavery International etc.

The attentions of these groups are by no means limited to how companies treat their own people. They draw no distinction between the treatment of people who are employed by the brand-holding company and those employed by the many companies in its supply chain. In the same way that a brand is held responsible for the quality of a final product, pressure groups advocate that the brand is equally responsible for the people who make the product. Within companies, these groups have engaged with public relations and corporate governance executives. Many TU leaders are concerned that as lead players, these groups are challenging their role in defending workers' rights.

With 1970s-style labour relations left behind, trade disputes are no longer about bringing down companies. Future jobs and working conditions of union members are more closely associated with corporate success than revolution. For example, TUs will concern themselves with job security in one company and in another, how the benefits of success should be shared. The unions have matured and have become partners rather than opponents. Conversely, nothing would give certain groups more pleasure than seeing Nike or Gap products boycotted or McDonald's golden arches crumble.

This new challenge matters only if company and brand reputations are damaged to the extent that sales volumes are affected. This occurs if customers feel strongly enough about people management issues to let them influence purchasing decisions.

Surveys conducted by Mori between 1999 and 2002 reveal:

- 7 out of 10 British people think business does not pay enough attention to social responsibility.
- 9 out of 10 people take CSR into account when forming a decision about a product or service.

The top three factors influencing a purchasing decision are:

- 98% quality
- 98% value for money
- 97% customer service

These are followed by:

- 83% treatment of employees
- 82% convenience
- 79% environment

Bob Haas, the Chief Executive of Levi Strauss, recently confirmed the effectiveness of the pressure group strategies when he said: 'A TV exposure on working conditions can undo years of effort to build brand loyalty.'

In a Washington Post article, Nike acknowledged that deterioration in its financial performance has been partly a result of 'resistance by consumers because of persistent allegations that the company mistreated factory workers'.

The speed and energy demonstrated by the world's coffee and chocolate manufacturers when responding to recent allegations of child and forced labour in African coffee plantations is further evidence of how seriously companies are taking these matters.

Adapted from People Management 2003

Required

The director of a large national organisation is concerned as a result of reading this article. As the newly appointed management consultant you have been asked to prepare are report outlining the following:

(a) The issue of **corporate social responsibility** including an argument against adopting social responsibility. (25 marks)

(b) How the organisation can become more socially responsible. (12 marks)

(c) **Ethical dilemmas** faced by a multi-national organisation. (13 marks)

(50 marks)

Answer Bank

1 Participation

Introduction

Some decisions may need to be made by an individual. However, decision makers are more often part of a group and effective decision-making often depends on whether the right people are involved in the right way in helping solve problems *Vroom*). As situations vary, decisions may warrant a style moving along a continuum ranging from **highly autocratic** to **highly democratic**. However, the appropriate amount of participation is more difficult to gauge as the personal decision style among those involved in decision making may be different with respect to how they perceive problems and make decisions (*Daft*). While there are some advantages to a participative style there are also some disadvantages as can be seen below.

Disadvantages of participative style

- **The degree of participation can vary**. A consultative or democratic style of leadership allows more participation than autocratic eg a manager might intend to allow participation to a limited extent, but still have the final say. However, some subordinates expect greater participation in the decision making process.

- A manager might be able to adopt a **participative style**, but be unable to reward subordinates for their work. If there is no progress from more effort to more rewards, subordinates may quickly lose interest and motivation.

- While joint decision-making can enhance member satisfaction and support a possibly risky decision, **not all people necessarily want to participate in decision-making** and some might be content to accept orders.

- While groups bring together a broader perspective for defining problems and diagnosing underlying causes and effects, **group decisions tend to be time-consuming** as people must be consulted and jointly diagnose problems and discuss solutions.

- **Groups may offer** more knowledge and facts with which to identify potential solutions and offer alternatives however, **a compromised solution** that is less than optimal for the organisation may be reached eg individuals might be motivated to consider the interests of their own group without having loyalty for the organisation as a whole.

- The **phenomenon of 'groupthink' is a potential barrier** as members can become so committed to a cohesive in-group that they may be reluctant to express contrary opinions and realistically consider alternatives (*Irving*).

- While people involved in decision-making may feel more satisfied and more likely to support the decisions made, **people do not want to be seen to be disagreeing with one another**. Thus the diversity of opinions essential to effective decision-making could be lost.

- While joint decisions can reduce uncertainty for those unwilling to undertake risks by themselves, there is **no clear focus of decision responsibility** or accountability.

- **Some work does not lend itself to a participative style** eg highly programmed routine work. In such work, decisions will be programmed or automatic and therefore participation in decision-making may be futile.

- **There could be disagreements between subordinates.** Some decisions may not be reached by common agreement. In such cases, the people losing the argument might resent the decision which is taken against them and might try to sabotage subsequent activities in order to prove themselves right.

Minimisation of disadvantages

The disadvantages of a participative style of management might be overcome as follows.

- The **extent of participation should be established clearly** so that everyone understands ie the leadership style should be consistent.
- **Authority should be delegated sufficiently** to enable small groups to take decisions about matters that are of some interest to them. One way of doing this in a large organisation might be to split the organisation up into many semi-independent divisions, and to encourage decentralisation within each division.
- **Re-structure jobs** so as to provide challenging work for work groups.
- **The participative style should be promoted by senior management** and implemented throughout the organisation, provided that the circumstances allow this to be one without adverse consequences.
- **Managers should be given powers to reward or punish subordinates**, so that subordinates will believe that by making more contributions to group discussions they will eventually receive fair reward.

Conclusion

Senior managers must pay careful attention to co-ordination of the goals and activities of sub-units within the organisation. These goals should be made clear to all employees and decisions by groups should be taken after giving full consideration to the needs of the organisation.

A procedure for resolving inter-group differences should be provided. Likert suggests the idea of a linking pin in which the leader of one group is a participating member of a more senior group, so that there is a continual overlap throughout the organisation. The ultimate task of co-ordination would be carried out at Board level.

2 Motivation

Introduction

Motivation is essential if you are to get the 'best' performance from any team. It affects both what individuals do but more importantly their attitude to doing it. Front line employees in particular who are in direct contact with customers have to be motivated to deliver a quality service and 'care' about the customers.

Theories of motivation

Because motivation is so important to the **effectiveness of a team**, it has attracted a lot of attention from management writers. Through his research, *Herzberg* has identified two types of factors relevant in employment situations. These are: **hygiene factors** eg pay and working conditions (lighting, heating and safety), and **motivator factors** eg challenging work; achievement, recognition from others; opportunities for advancement and promotion, etc. Managers must first ensure that the hygiene factors are in place and then consider positive motivators as mentioned above. It should be remembered that what motivates one person will not necessarily motivate another.

Drucker, however, is critical of Hertzberg's theory as the focus is on **job satisfaction** as opposed to **job dissatisfaction**. He suggests that motivation through employee satisfaction is a 'wishy-washy' idea, as it has no particular meaning and feels satisfaction comes about by encouraging employees to accept **responsibility**.

Maslow (as seen in the diagram below) through his research into the human potential for growth identified a hierarchy of motivation needs. He suggests people strive to fulfil their needs from the most basic **physiological needs** necessary for survival to the level of **self-actualisation**. He argues that when a level of need is fulfilled, an individual is no longer motivated by them but will move to the next level as these will now be motivating. These needs include **psychological needs** for social acceptance and personal achievement and a sense of belonging; development of self-esteem through recognition, status, approval, achievement and prestige and self-fulfilment through enriching experiences at the level of self-actualisation which means to actualise, or realise, all of one's unique potential.

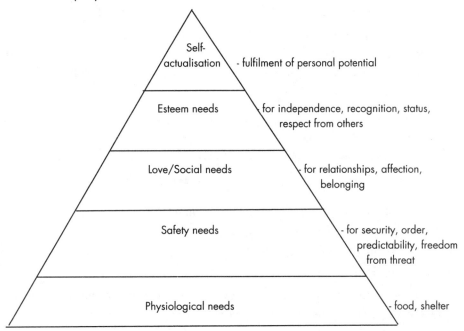

Criticsm of Maslow's work suggests this does not always hold true for everyone as more than one level of need can be experienced at the same time and people could have different priorities of needs; it is **culture bound** as the assumptions may be restricted to a highly rational, materialistic and individualistic Western culture and, some cultures operate on the premise that the welfare of the group (belongingness needs) is more highly valued than the needs of the individual (esteem needs).

The hierarchy does indicate however that managers have to think about changing the motivators used. As employees move through the hierarchy eg at low levels they may be motivated by money, but at higher levels, status and recognition of peers, time off or other rewards like job security may be more effective.

What works?

The most effective motivator **will depend on the individual and his or her needs at that time** eg a poor student working in catering may be effectively motivated by financial rewards (tips) to offer high levels of customer care, while a manager may be motivated by **recognition and achievement**.

In sales teams, motivational schemes are often fairly sophisticated, with **rewards** on the 'Best' sales person, incentive gifts, prizes and competitions. This is necessary to get over the particular problems of employees working in isolation, often away from direct support.

In other cases individuals are motivated by the possibility of **advancement and status**, like those motivated to study for CIM examinations. **Participation and involvement** in work or a project can also act as a powerful motivator. Teams that are involved and committed to an objective or vision are often highly successful.

It is the job of the manager to find out what motivates employees in any particular environment or situation, and to take action to devise positive schemes to motivate them and facilitate their **growth in the job**.

3 New product development team

> *Tutorial note.* The approach to the answer should have been:
>
> - Carry out an audit/assessment of the skills required
> - Set objectives
> - Consider team structure
> - Manage and monitor progress
>
> Consider developing relationships between departments, the structure and size of teams, and team-building activities.

MEMO

To: Team Leader, New Product Development
From: Marketing Manager
Date: 1 March 20X2
Subject: Effective teams

As the new team leader for product development, you asked me for my advice and comments on effective performance. I outline my comments below.

(a) **Audit of current situation**

First of all, it is necessary to carry out an audit of the situation you face. This means assessing the following.

- The level of cross-functional skills present
- The size and authority level of the team
- The objectives you have been set
- An analysis of the task itself
- The timescales involved
- The personalities, experience and attitudes of team members
- Methods of auditing team members
- The level of budget and resources allocated to the task

Expanding on some of these points will help you evaluate the way that the team should perform best to be successful.

(i) **Cross functional skills**

There is strong evidence to link successful new product development with empowered, multi-functional teams. There will need to be effective interfaces between departments such as research and development, marketing, operations, purchasing and finance. You need to establish that there is a balance of critical activities that fall into the necessary different functional areas of the business.

(ii) **Authority and resources**

Find out how much authority the team has to make decisions, what resources have been allocated to ensure success, and how much time each member is given to devote to the team exercise away from their present job.

(iii) **Timescales**

Understand how much time you have to build your team. This will show how much priority you should give to the stages of team promotion and development. Normally, one of the most critical success factors in new product development is the speed to market, and organisational development is the biggest factor in cycle time reduction.

(iv) **Team members and auditing them**

This needs to be done in a similar way to a selection process for a new recruit, but in a more informal way internally. You could, for example, ask to see their appraisal records and look at the their personnel files.

Finally, you should hold one to one interviews with each prospective team member, to gauge their reaction to joining the team, and the sort of role they would be most suited to.

(b) **Recommendations**

It is important to understand that an effective team is one with a common commitment, and focused on a common purpose, with a set of performance goals to which they are mutually accountable. This then is the aim you should work towards, and in doing so you should aim to create the following characteristics.

- Working towards clear objectives
- Open relationships between team members
- Encouragement of debate and deal with different viewpoints
- Clear and identifiable allocation of tasks
- Develop personal relationships based on personal knowledge and trust
- Ensure members show each other a high level of support
- Work through and resolve conflicts
- Establish effective procedures and decision making processes
- Have a skilful leader who is appropriate to the rest of the team

(i) **Team leader**

Before looking at individual aspects, you should be aware of your role as team leader. Leadership is simply the ability to influence people towards the attainment of goals. There is no one style of leadership, as each of us has personal strengths we can develop but in this sense I assume the team is a horizontal one with responsible people from a range of disciplines.

You will therefore need to encourage freedom of expression and creativity. This must be tempered with decisiveness and a focus on achieving the objectives.

Team leaders should also manage the process of team development successfully, as colleagues get to know each other, conflicts emerge which need to be resolved, and the team eventually settles together to become committed to achieving tasks.

Leadership of the team may need to vary in some circumstances when you need certain specialists to assume control of the part of the task which is in their main functional responsibility.

(ii) **Objectives**

Once the team is together, you need to identify and focus on the task and objectives for new product development. As well as the broad company objectives, you should draw up a more specific task description which expands on the overall task, breaking it down into separate identifiable 'SMART' objectives which all members can agree and relate to. These objectives would also set criteria for successful completion, which then allows for feedback and modification as necessary.

(iii) **Team members**

You should evaluate the members of the team, and their strengths and weaknesses. A successful team leader works towards people's strengths, and allows them roles to which they are most suited.

You must assess the size of the team and the skills needed. The larger the team, the greater scope for conflict and loss of direction. Between 7 and 12 members would probably give the right spread of experience and skills.

Once the team is together, you should acknowledge and recognise people's strengths and skills in front of other members. This will help develop respect for each other.

(iv) **Team tasks and roles**

A key aspect of teamwork is to allocate tasks to the right individuals once you have identified the objectives and therefore tasks to be carried out. These tasks will be functional at first. As the dynamics of the team develop, you will find members naturally fit into certain roles which best suit their strengths. These roles will include specialist roles for opinions, seeking information, summarising, monitoring and enthusiastic stimulation. Roles will also include emotional ones which support members' needs and help to strengthen team bonds.

Your team will also need a strong element of creativity and innovation present to back up the elements of task completion and organisation.

At this stage you can also assess any training needs.

(v) **Team building**

You also need to find ways to create harmony and opportunities for members to get to know each other. This is often best achieved outside the work environment, organising social get togethers or team games, etc, which help foster a team spirit.

An important way to motivate the team is to acknowledge success for each task completed.

(vi) **Communication**

Teamwork is all about communication. As well as the interpersonal aspects, it is important that you establish clear lines and methods of communication to keep people informed of progress, and task allocation, timescales etc.

Finally, remember to ensure that the company is helping the team by working to the following roles for successful teams in new product development.

- Dedicated and focused team
- Team given accountability for the whole project from start to finish
- The team members devote a large percentage of time to the project
- Top management has given strong support and commitment

I wish you luck in your new position, and hope that my comments are helpful.

4 Planning a team

To: Joseph Spangler, CEO, Xpressions Unlimited
From: Sean Patrick, Dynamic Management Consultancy
Subject: Planning a Team
Date: 11th July 20X1

Introduction

The purpose of any team is that **the sum of the collective output far outweighs that of individuals working in isolation**. However, simply bringing a group of individuals together does not make a team. A crucial ingredient to the overall effectiveness of a team requires synergy. For effectiveness, tasks that deal with complex problems require specific people with specific skills and perspectives to work together to develop a solution. With the aim of bringing together complimentary skills, there is a need to select the right individuals before the team can be formed and developed.

Selecting a Team

If you are faced with starting a team from scratch, you begin by identifying what the task is and what skills are needed to achieve the objectives. Hereafter, group members can be identified from within or outside the organisation.

In today's business approach of **flatter matrix organisations**, the formation of teams for relatively short periods is becoming more common. These so-called **project teams** bring together individuals from different disciplines, backgrounds and even different companies. The project manager therefore has two key roles:

- Selecting the right mix of individuals.
- Actively working to turn individuals into an effective team in as short a time as possible.

In general, common sense would suggest that the best members of a team are those that generate the best results. In practice, this is not always the case. A team drawn from a combination of team role descriptions should be developed to embrace both the technical competences needed to fulfil relevant tasks and balanced functional roles in task performance and team maintenance: leaders; idea generators; critical evaluators; organisers; mediators; resource mobilisers etc.

This is borne out by *Belbin*, who concludes that the most consistently successful groups comprise a range of roles undertaken by various members. According to him, individuals have preferred roles and therefore, to be effective, they should be given tasks to allow them to operate in their preferred role. These roles can be seen in the table below.

Type	Typical Features
Co-ordinator/Chairman	Presides and co-ordinates; balanced, disciplined, good at working through others.
Shaper	Highly strung, dominant, dynamic, extrovert, passionate about the task itself.
Implementer/Company Worker	Practical organiser, turning ideas into tasks – scheduling, planning etc trustworthy and efficient; not a leader, but an administrator.
Monitor/Evaluator	Analytically (rather than creatively intelligent), dissects ideas, spots flaws, possibly aloof.
Plant	Introverted, but intellectually dominant and imaginative, a source of ideas for the group.
Resource Investigator	Popular, sociable, extrovert, relaxed; source of new contacts, but not an originator.
Team Worker	Most concerned with team maintenance; supportive, understanding, diplomatic, popular but uncompetitive.
Completer-finisher	Chivvies the team to meet deadlines, attends to details, and follows things through; not always popular.
Specialist	Provides knowledge and technical skills within the team. They may be introverted and anxious but tend to be self-starting, dedicated and committed.

Where there is an uneven spread of roles in a group their may be problems in addressing the task allocated. Belbin suggests two or three shapers, in a group, for example, can lead to conflict and inner fighting. Therefore, team members need to be aware of their main team role, know their second best role and see if these can compliment the others in the group. In this way, an effective team can be constructed. If there are too many 'shapers' and 'plants' and not enough or no 'completer finishers' or 'monitor/evaluators', there is likely to be too much talking and no follow-through of actions or balance and reality brought to the proceedings.

Team development

Groups do not come into teams fully formed. *Tuckman* suggests that groups pass through five stages of development as can be seen below.

- **Forming** – when individuals in the groups start to find out about other members of the group and are keen to impress. Usually look to a leader for guidance about the nature of the task.

- **Storming** – A stage of conflict. Members bargain amongst themselves while sorting out their personal goals and that of the group. If members' goals are conflicting, hostility may break out and resist the control of other members.

- **Norming** – Group members develop harmony having established responsibilities and information is freely passed between group members.

- **Performing** – Having developed cohesion, the group experiences commitment to problem solving and accomplishing the stated objectives.

- **Adjourning/mourning** – The group disbands when the task has been achieved or members leave.

Pace of progress through all stages may be varied depending on the composition of the team, capabilities of the members and the task at hand. Some groups may get stuck at the storming stage and therefore remain inefficient.

Team building activities

Particularly when a team is new, or to maintain cohesion, teambuilding activities should be undertaken. Some activities are listed below.

- **Icebreaking and role development exercises** eg outdoor events, sports and social activities.
- **Positive inter-team competitions** with rewards for high performing teams or team suggestions.
- **Intra-team mentoring and coaching programmes** to encourage appreciation of each other's roles.
- **Team presentations** on key issues to other teams and senior management.

The benefit of team building events are important and will require systematic planning and budgeting, monitoring and evaluating.

5 Leadership and performance

> *Tutorial note.* This question requires you to justify the importance of effective leadership: you are not asked to discuss or differentiate between different leadership theories or styles, although you may refer briefly to theory to explain what effective leadership consists of. Note the key 'instruction' phrases in the question: 'individual, team and business performance' and 'particularly from a customer perspective'.

MEMORANDUM

From: Your Name, Marketing Manager
To: The Management Team
Date: Today's date
Re: Leadership

Following our discussions last week on recent signs of poor performance and staff demotivation, I have compiled some thoughts, as requested, on the problem of poor leadership and how more effective leadership could improve individual, team and business performance.

1 **What is effective leadership?**

   The distinction between 'management' and 'leadership' arose out of a recognition that 'the essence of leadership is followership. In other words, it is the willingness of people to follow that makes a person a leader'. (*Koontz, O'Donnell, Weihrich*) Time, projects and activities can be managed; only people can be led. Effective leaders exercise interpersonal and influencing skills to gain what *Katz and Kahn* call 'the influential increment over and above mechanical compliance with the routine directives of the organisation'. Effective leaders are also the creators and sellers of cultural values in the organisation.

2 **Why is leadership important for our business?**

   Leadership skills are particularly important in business environments such as printing, where there is intense competition for a small pool of skilled labour and a corresponding demand for quality of working life. Leadership, by inspiring and persuading, is more appealing than a command-and-control style of management. At the same time, small print businesses like ours are constantly under pressure from bigger competitors and the pace of technological change. In such an environment, employee commitment is essential in order to facilitate change and innovation: leaders are better placed to address change and crisis management issues and to encourage a culture of flexibility, co-operation and creative thinking.

3 **How can leadership improve performance?**

Effective leadership can improve performance - particularly from the customers' perspective - in the following ways.

(a) Leadership inspires staff to **commitment**, rather than mere **compliance**. Guest (*Employment Relations*) considers that a commitment-based system of control has significant advantages over a compliance-based system, in terms of loyalty, adaptability, performance improvement and utilisation of resources (at an individual, team and business level). Compliance by definition goes no further than what is laid down by the rules: the taking of responsibility and initiative to act in response to specific (potentially unforeseen) customer demands is the product of commitment.

(b) Leadership directs employees' energies towards the company's **mission and objectives** (rather than existing rules and procedures) and so gives permission for thinking outside the box. This allows creativity and entrepreneurship in pursuit of continual improvement in products and services to customers.

(c) Leadership facilitates self-responsibility and self-management in individuals and teams, as it is respectful and empowering of employees' capabilities, aspirations and efforts.

   (i) This offers a non-aversive form of discipline and morale, and the motivating opportunity for recognition and self-actualisation. Improved motivation in turn impacts favourably on individual and team performance: reducing errors, increasing output and encouraging positive attitudes in customer relations.

   (ii) It also allows for more efficient and flexible use of the human resource, which improves business performance. From the customers' perspective, this may be experienced as a more flexible experience of the company, with few structural barriers created by functional demarcations and rules.

   (iii) Self-responsibility and initiative also facilitates front-line problem-solving and action to meet customer needs, without lead times for consultation and authorisation.

(d) Leadership is one of the key factors in *Handy's* **contingency theory of effective group performance**. Effective team-working in turn facilitates delivery of customer expectations, through more contributive problem-solving and performance synergy. Leadership facilitates co-operative team-working by:

   (i) Focusing the team's energies on shared goals and outputs rather than on roles, rules and job descriptions, allowing more creative collaboration (for example, multi-skilling, brainstorming, increased communication and so on)

   (ii) Managing differences and potential conflicts within the group based on shared commitment and the interpersonal skills of the leader rather than grievance mechanisms

   (iii) Championing the team and mobilising resources on behalf of its efforts

(e) At the level of business performance, leadership does three other things.

   (i) It suits the expectations and aspirations of today's highly skilled, flexible and mobile labour, allowing us to attract and retain the specialist staff we need to meet customer demands

   (ii) It fosters a strong corporate culture, which allows the organisation to present a positive and coherent corporate identity or 'brand' in the marketplace, and gives customers a positive and consistent experience of the company

   (iii) It creates vision and values for the company: for which, quality will be key from the customers' perspective

Conclusion

The idea that leaders are born, not made no longer holds credibility in organisational theory. Modern theories suggest that effective leadership can be adopted as a 'style' or learned as a body of functional skills. I recommend that we investigate the many leadership training programmes available, with a view to accessing the benefits outlined above.

6 Emotional intelligence

Introduction

The shift in economy away from manufacturing to services in the UK in the latter part of the 20th Century **to knowledge-based** forms of employment in the early 21st Century, has forced changes for many people. Along with this, the technological revolution is said to be de-humanising the work force and preventing personal interaction with one another. Many organisations have restructured or folded, placing societies under considerable strain. Stress and absence from the workplace is said to be on the increase and thus many individuals are addressing their **work/life balance**. In light of the above, people have faced enormous change. However, different individuals possess different strengths and weakness in their ability to adapt.

Emotional Intelligence (EQ)

As emotions control and drive behaviour, the choice is to decide whether to fight emotions or work with them to achieve goals ie to go against the flow one may risk certain consequences of self-destruction eg embarrassment or regret.

Wood & Tolley suggest it is possible to break EQ down into the following components or competences:

- **Self-regulation** – Being able to manage your own emotional state ie
  - Defer judgement; curb impulse
  - Detach yourself
  - Express yourself, but do it assertively not aggressively
  - Be flexible; go with the flow; don't force things

- **Self-awareness** – Awareness of your own feelings and of how others respond to you, ie
  - Respect yourself
  - Be positive
  - Be true to yourself
  - Give logic and rationality a rest
  - Listen to others
  - Understand your impact on others

- **Motivation** – energising and directing behaviour through channelling your emotions and the ability to pursue longer-term goals, ie
    - Striving to improve and achieve high standards
    - Being committed to achieving your goals
    - Taking the initiative and seizing opportunities
    - Being optimistic even in the face of adversity
- **Empathy** – The ability to recognise and read emotions in others, ie
    - Being sensitive towards and understanding others
    - Making the needs and interest of others your point of reference
    - Furthering the development of other people
    - Being socially and politically tuned in
- **Social skills** – relating to and influencing others, ie
    - Developing and sustaining interpersonal relationships
    - Communicating with others
    - Working with others

Wood and Tolley also suggest, while these components are interconnected in a complex manner, the ability to perform effectively in any one, is closely related to how capable one is in the others.

The influence of EQ on a manager's skills

Goleman argues **'leadership is not about domination**, but the art of persuading people to work towards a common goal'. A number of management writers concur that EQ is at a premium amongst leaders and managers today and suggest what is missing in the work environment is **good interpersonal skills**.

An emotionally intelligent manager will:

- Understand their own inner feelings and be able to appreciate other's points of view and therefore be able to **stay on an 'even-keel'** ie they have to understand themselves before they can understand others (self-awareness).

- **Be able to sense and anticipate a likely response** to any suggestions and engage in a considerate, mature and pleasant way (empathy).

- Will **possess 'people skills'** ie will be capable of motivating others; offer personal and social competence; be skilled in all aspects of empathy and in possession of a full range of social skills (motivation).

- Have good self-regulation allowing them to function effectively ie will manage their own feelings so that they **behave in a manner that is appropriate to the circumstances** (self-regulation).

- Will **question their assumptions, listen attentively to what people are saying and observe how they are behaving** in order to fine-tune their responses to them (social skills).

Conclusion

In today's climate of constant change, communication and good interpersonal skills are of key importance and allow for feelings and emotions to be expressed. *McGregor* states that 'groups function best when everyone speaks their mind; when people listen as well as speak; when disagreements surface without causing obvious tensions; when the 'chairman of the board' does not try to dominate his subordinates; and when decisions rest on consensus'. Goleman points out, one cannot suddenly become emotionally smart therefore, **anything that brings the best out in others is to be sought and cultivated**.

7 Marketing task

Introduction

Marketers are facing a number of new strategic challenges as the environment changes. These include increasing pressure from governments to take a greater account of green, consumer and community relations issues, the growing power of global companies and concentration of power within industries, changing social and cultural trends which bring about fragmentation of markets and innovation based on new technologies and emergent industries which stem from this.

The focus of this question will be on the last two of these issues; market fragmentation and, shorter and less predictable life cycles. The cause of these changes is discussed and how they affect the practice of marketing.

Market fragmentation

People today are more eclectic in taste and style. For example, on occasion they may indulge in fast food while their staple diet is one of health consciousness. Only a few years ago there was a limited access to news and information. Today there is a plethora of terrestrial, satellite and cable channels most of which are interactive to choose from and also, there is the opportunity to read any one of hundreds of newspapers or magazines, listen to any of the myriad of radio stations or search for a particular topic on the Internet.

Shorter and less predictable product life cycles

These are a characteristic of high technology products and services. New technology and innovations have escalated over the last 30 years, with new products, concepts, channels and technology being launched at a massive rate. High technology products almost have a built in obsolescence, as technology development never stays still. Predicting the diffusion of innovation rate is very difficult.

Causes of market fragmentation and lack of predictability of life cycles

- **Social change**

    The CIM/Henley Centre report, '*Metamorphosis in Marketing*' details how consumer behaviour and attitudes are changing, as are traditional consumer life stages. *Wells and Gube's* traditional family life cycle model which depicts a staged progression from youth to marriage and family to empty nesters is now a much less predictable path.

    Trends in social change in the UK show: a career for life is no longer the norm; redundancies and self-employment are rising; a growing number of women in the workplace resulting in rising affluence of women; increase in divorce rate; more people caring for elderly parents and an increase in middle age inheritances. All of these factors disrupt the traditional pattern and lead to **more consumer segments** in many markets. The growth in 'minority' lifestyles is creating opportunities for niche brands aimed at consumers with very distinct purchasing habits.

- **Technological innovation**

    This is bringing the ability to create **large numbers of product variants** without corresponding increases in resources and causing markets to become overcrowded. The

fragmentation of the media to service ever more specialist and local audiences is denying mass media the ability to assure market dominance for major brand advertisers. This creates space for **niche players** and **speeds up the diffusion of innovation** thus shortening life cycles. The advance in information technology is enabling information about individual customers to be organised in ways that enable highly selective and personal communications. It also fuels quicker 'me-too' product launches that potentially **shorten product life cycles**.

How should the marketing manager respond to these challenges?

Finer segmentation, in response to market fragmentation, looks certain to play an even more crucial role in the marketing strategies in the years ahead. The move from traditional mass marketing to **'micro marketing'** is rapidly gaining ground as marketers explore the incremental profit potential of niche markets.

Perhaps the most important response has to come in relation to long-term marketing strategy. With less predictable life cycles, marketing managers must **redefine the guidelines** provided by the traditional PLC. In order for PLC theory to be relevant, some kind of reliable method for projecting life spans of the product is needed. With technology advancing so rapidly, historical data is no longer sufficient to be a useful predictive tool. It has been suggested that the concept of the Technology Life Cycle is superior to the PLC concept. A key difference in thinking is that high-tech organisations must **make a critical decision regarding focus**. A company can attempt to follow a technology through its life cycle or specialise in one stage. Whichever is chosen, **speed of response** becomes vital.

I think *Hooley and Saunders* suggest that in **fragmented markets** success depends on finding niches where particular product specifications are needed, as in the computer software market. As each niche provides little opportunity for growth, an organisation needs to **find a number of niches** with some degree of commonality, to allow economies of scale to be achieved.

In contrast to **niche players**, brands such as Marks and Spencer and McDonald's over-arch social differences and appeal to standard needs on an international scale. As such, marketers have to stretch their vision to encompass the details and speed of **micro-marketing** and rapid new product development, global branding, the cost pressures of tertiary brands and the image and service pressures of having a differentiated offering.

8 Champion of change

To: David Roy, CEO, P. W. Storey Ltd
From: Felicity Hayward. Management Consultant
Subject: Change Management Process
Date: 12 April 20X7

1.0 Introduction

Handy suggests there is one constant in life, and that is **change.** As you have already identified, the organisation has little choice as to whether to change or not. The intention therefore, is to highlight the **forces for change**; causes of resistance to change and make recommendations for managing the process of change.

2.0 Forces for change and causes of resistance

2.1 Forces for change – internal

- Poor operational performance
- High costs
- Low productivity

2.2 Forces for change - external

- Competition from foreign, subsidised steel makers
- High export prices caused by appreciation of the domestic currency
- Weak domestic demand for steel
- Customer complaints

2.3 Forces resisting change - internal

- Long-serving managers' complacency
- The trade unions attitude
- Parochial self-interest
- Misunderstanding
- Different assessments of the situation
- People's low tolerance of change

2.4 Forces resisting change - external

- Growing demand in Pacific rim countries

3.0 Managing the process of change

Recommendations are made as follows:

- *Lewin* suggests that after the forces for and against change have been established, effort should be put not only into breaking down those opposing it (which is a natural management response), but also into building up the influence of those supporting it.

- Application of the *Lewin/Schein* change model suggests moving through a **process of changing states**. These are: **'unfreeze'**, **'moving'** and **'refreezing'**. In line with this, in the first phase (unfreeze), a programme of education and support will have to be set up for the complacent managers. **Negotiations** will also have to be entered into with the respective trade unions. The basic aim is to enlighten both parties with evidence showing potential looming disaster as is clearly shown by the organisation's current competitive situation. This transparency can alleviate an early crisis and can trigger a willingness to change.

- The **'moving' phase** is essentially the process of making the actual changes that will move the organisation to the new state. This will also involve new types of behaviour (including new patterns and reinforcing them) by individuals. It is therefore recommended that residual resistance should be confronted with free circulation of information (eg intranet, monthly newsletter etc) about plans for the future and why they are required. Some individuals may need more assistance than others to embrace change eg counselling may be necessary to help an individual to come to terms with changing attitudes and behaviours. An extensive **programme of organisational development** is thus likely to be required. In doing so, it is essential that proper application of positive and negative reinforcement in the shape of rewards and sanctions are made.

- During the final phase of **'refreeze'**, employees should be prevented from slipping back into their old ways and attitudes by a combination of exhortation, reward for good performance and sanctions against the backsliders.
- While **external forces** are less susceptible to this treatment than internal ones, representations could be made to government about both the exchange rate and the unfair competition. This can be undertaken through a trade association or other umbrella body (eg the CBI). However, it is necessary to recognise that even if action is forthcoming, it is unlikely to be prompt.

I trust that this report will sufficiently assist in managing the process of change within your organisation. If you have any further queries, please do not hesitate to contact me.

9 Marketing orientation

Introduction

In market-led organisations, the marketing department is not in a world of it's own. Customer value is designed and created by multi-function product teams supporting all the business functions. Therefore, by creating a culture that is wholly customer-focused, delivering superior customer value to internal (employees) and external (customers), the primary objective is to achieve a market orientation in order to facilitate a competitive advantage and ultimately prosper.

Developing market orientation

Hooley et al have identified the following components as a way of achieving market orientation.

- Customers – Know them well enough to give superior value.
- Competition - What are their short- and long-term capabilities?
- Long-term profit focus – Have a strategic but realistic vision.
- Inter-functional – Mobilise the entire organisation to create superior customer value.
- Culture – Employee behaviour should be managed to ensure customer satisfaction.

Drummond and Ensor elaborate on this and suggest the following.

Customer focused

There is a need to understand the organisation's customer base and be responsive to their needs. Loyal customers should be **treated as assets**, customer retention and satisfaction should be **monitored** and the aim should be to strive towards building on-going and long-term relationships. To this end, markets need to be defined, customers **listened to** and customers effectively **segmented/targeted.**

Competitor focused

Competitors must be observed and their objectives, strategies and capabilities assessed. Their products, processes and operations must be benchmarked against the organisation's own.

Long-term profit focus

A market-orientated long-term strategic vision needs to be developed through viewing marketing as more than a series of promotional tools and techniques. Senior management should develop and implement market-led strategy and define the future in terms of creating long-term value for stakeholders.

Inter-functional

Marketing should not be confined to the marketing department and should be integrated into the business. Every function and individual within the organisation has a role to play in creating value and achieving the goal of being a market-led organisation. However, this may require fundamental changes in the organisation's culture and structure.

Culture

Unless employees buy-in to the new strategic vision through commitment to a common vision, then it is highly unlikely that the organisation will become truly market orientated. Therefore, there may be a need to overcome barriers. Some of these are:

- **Poor internal communications** – It is essential to have a culture that reinforces and models open and honest communications 'top down and bottom up'. By sharing feelings and beliefs, employees can form a clear picture of their leaders' values and priorities. Success is dependent on the ability to share values across the organisation.

- **Fear of change** – Individuals dislike change. Stepping out of their comfort zone makes them feel insecure and uncertain. This can interfere with their social structure and their relationship with others.

- **Insufficient resources** –Insufficient investment eg time and money, could hinder implementation of strategic plans for the future development of the organisation thus failing to meet objectives ie the impact of which could result in failing to become truly market orientated.

A technique used to overcome these barriers is **internal marketing**. It is the use of a marketing approach in the internal environment of an organisation, whose employees who are seen as customers and have to be persuaded to buy into management ideas.

Internal marketing

Just as the normal processes of marketing outside the organisation are determined by a marketing plan, so too should the process of internal marketing be subject to an **internal marketing plan**. This can be achieved through the use of the internal marketing mix: segmentation, product, price, place and promotion.

- **Segmentation** – Employees can be segmented in the same way as external marketing. Different criteria can be used eg management or department level. For example, British Aerospace embarked on a major culture change strategy and identified senior managers who had to be convinced of the need for the new approach. This could be simply defined as segmenting the individuals into categories 'for' the new strategy, 'against' and 'neutrals'.

- **Product** – This is the plan or change which management wants to implement.

- **Price** – The cost or price that employees will have to pay. This can be measured as: loss of status; uncertainty; stress, etc.

- **Place** – The way of getting the plan to employees eg seminars; training; team briefings conducted in the appropriate time frame.

- **Promotion** – Poor communication is probably the biggest single internal problem. The grapevine tends to work quickly and not always accurately. Good communication is essential to ensure the plans are owned and supported by all employees. Methods of communication include: presentations; reports; in-house magazines; intranet; team briefings; notice boards etc. Feedback should be encouraged at every opportunity.

Implementation

To ensure effective implementation, it is vital that a task force or project team who possess the necessary project management skills are selected. For example:

- They are capable of setting **SMART objectives**.
- They have the ability to **break down a plan** into smaller manageable tasks.
- They have the ability to **delegate**.
- They have the capability of **effective team building**.
- They have the ability to **respond quickly and effectively** to unforeseen crisis.

Conclusion

Even effective use of inwardly directed marketing techniques cannot solve all employee related quality and customer satisfaction problems. Research has shown that actions by Human Resource Departments or effective programmes of recruitment, training and development, are likely to be more effective than marketing-based activities. Therefore, rather than internal marketing, external recruitment could be the solution ie selecting the right individual to fit into the new culture. However, the internal marketing concept does have a major role to play in making employees more customer-focused.

10 Change and the individual

To: The Managing Director, Mentoes plc
From: Megan Lyn, HR Manager
Subject: Change and The Individual
Date: 16 July 200X

1.0 Introduction

"Forces that operate to bring about change in organisations can be thought of as winds which are many and varied – from small summer breezes which merely disturb a few papers to mighty howling gales which cause devastation to structures and operations causing consequent reorientation of purpose and rebuilding' (Senior).

2.0 The drivers of change

The metaphorical winds are in fact the external and internal drivers of change. These include:

- **External factors**

    PESTEL factors (political, economic, social, technological, environmental and legal) eg information technology; changing employee demographics; performance gaps; government regulation; global economic competition etc.

- **Internal factors**

    These may include internal technical or administrative changes, financial and social developments eg unskilled and semi-skilled jobs being automated; need for greater flexibility in the workforce; working at home; new leadership; shared employment etc.

3.0 The effect of change on individuals

Faced with change, individuals encounter all or some of the following.

- **Circumstantial change** - Living in a new house; establishing new relationships; working to new routines etc. This will involve letting go of things and learning new ways of doing things.

- **Physiological change** – This may be natural ie the ageing process or as a result of external factors as discussed above.

- **Psychological change**

    (i) **Disorientation** before new circumstances have been assimilated. A new set of models may have to be confronted if the change involves a new roles set, new milieux, new relationships.

    (ii) **Uncertainty** may lead to **insecurity**, especially acute in changes involving work (staying in employment) and/or fast acclimatisation (a short learning curve may lead to feelings of incapacity).

    (iii) New expectations, challenges and pressures may generate **role stress** in which an individual feels discomfort in the role he or she plays.

    (iv) **Powerlessness**. Change can be particularly threatening if it is perceived as an outside force or agent against which the individual is powerless.

Hayes refers to individual change as moving through **phases of transition** and suggests during the process, individuals experience a **variety of emotional and cognitive states** and progress typically through a cycle of reasonably predictable phases. These are described below.

- **Awareness/Shock** – Individuals often have little warning of changes and they experience the initial phase of a transition as a shock.

- **Denial** – This phase is characterised by a retreat from the reality of change. Negative changes may be denied or trivialised and attention may be displaced (avoidance strategy).

- **Depression** – Eventually the reality of change becomes apparent and the individual acknowledges that things cannot continue as they are.

- **Letting go** – This involves accepting reality for what it is; it implies a letting go of the past.

- **Testing** – A more active, creative, experimental involvement in the new situation starts to take place. New ways of behaving and being are tried out; more energy is available but anger and irritability may be easily aroused if the new behaviour is not successful.

- **Consolidation** – Out of the testing process come some new ways of being and behaving which are gradually adopted as new norms. It involves reflecting on new experiences and assessing whether they offer a basis for a constructive way forward and learning to build on this experience and informs the choice of future testing experiences.

- **Internalisation, reflection and learning** – The transition is complete when the changed behaviour is normal and unthinking and is the new natural order of things. It is at this point that learning and personal growth, which may benefit future transitions, is recognised.

Hayes further suggests, that the time taken to pass through the various phases will vary and there is a possibility that individuals may regress and slip back to an earlier stage in the process as they face up to new challenges. It should also be noted that some may get stuck at any phase and not complete this cycle.

4.0 Barriers to individual change

Greenberg says researchers have noted several key factors that are known to make individuals resistant to change in organisations and highlights these as:

- **Economic insecurity** - Any changes on the job have the potential to threaten one's livelihood by either loss of job or reduced pay and therefore, some resistance to change is inevitable.

- **Fear of the unknown** – Employees derive a sense of security from doing things the same way, knowing who their co-workers will be, and whom they are supposed to answer to from day to day. Disrupting these well-established, comfortable patterns creates unfamiliar conditions, a state of affairs that is often rejected.

- **Threats to social relationships** – As people continue to work within organisations, they form strong bonds with their co-workers. Many organisational changes threaten the integrity of friendship groups that provide valuable social rewards.

- **Habit** – Jobs that are well learned and become habitual are easy to perform. The prospect of changing the way a job is done challenges people to develop new job skills. Doing this is clearly more difficult than continuing to perform the job as it was originally learned.

- **Failure to recognise the need for change** – Unless employees recognise and fully appreciate the need for changes in organisations, any vested interested they may have in keeping things the same may overpower their willingness to accept change.

Conclusion

Employees who are involved in the change process are likely to be better able to understand the need for change and are therefore less likely to resist it.

11 Brand stretching

Introduction

A brand can be defined as a collection of attributes that strongly influence purchase (*Davidson*). Experts now view brands as the link between a company's marketing activities and consumers' perceptions of these activities. Since the 1990s this brand revolution has been particularly relevant to sectors such as financial services. The difficulties consumers have in understanding intangible products and the extent to which the service becomes the brand, both present marketing challenges together with the need to exploit **brand equity** through **brand stretching activities.** Therefore, there is a need to apply a **brand strategy process** that is one of the steps in the **brand planning process** as outlined below.

Elements of Brand Strategy

Arnold outlines a five stage brand management process.

Stage	Description
Market analysis	An overview of trends in the macro and micro-environment which includes customer and competitor analysis and the identification of any PEST factors likely to affect the brand. For soft drinks, the explosion of competitive activity, particularly by own label and new product introductions eg Lucazade will be important.
Brand situation analysis	Analysis of the brand's personality and individual attributes. This represents the internal audit and questions to be asked eg, 'Is advertising projecting the right image?; 'Is the packaging too aggressive? and 'Does the product need updating? This is a fundamental evaluation of the brand's character.
Targeting future positions	This is the core brand strategy. Any brand strategy could incorporate what has been learnt in stages (i) and (ii) above into a view of how the market will evolve and what strategic response is most appropriate. Brand strategy can be considered as follows. (a) Target markets (b) Brand positions (c) Brand scope
Testing new offers	Once the strategy has been decided the next step is to develop individual elements of the marketing mix and test the brand concept for clarity, credibility and competitiveness with the target market.
Planning and evaluating performance	The setting of the brand budget, establishing the type of support activity needed and measurement of results against objectives. Information on tracking of performance feeds into step (i) of the brand management process.

From this we see that brand strategy involves decision on three issues: **target market(s), brand positioning and brand stretching.**

Brand stretching

Brand stretching refers specifically to the use of an existing, successful brand being used to **launch products in an unrelated market**. A brand extension on the other hand, is using the same brand name, successfully established in one market or channelled to enter another similar market eg Virgin Financial Services are **stretched** into Virgin Trains and a brand extension could be Mars Bars into Mars ice cream.

For this strategy to be successful the current brand's **core values must be identified and be relevant** to the new market. The **new market area must not affect the core values of the brand by association** ie failure in one activity can adversely affect the core brand. For example, adverse publicity for Virgin Trains could damage the core values throughout the Virgin Group.

Another example would be Marks and Spencer with its retail operations. They have established a **strong brand image** for quality, value and integrity. All of which are important in the financial services market. This has allowed Marks and Spencer to stretch their brand successfully into the financial services sector.

There is a school of thought that states that it may be easier for service companies to stretch umbrella brands across markets. Financial services companies eg American Express, can utilise database-marketing programmes across their whole service range. In general though, most financial service brands are currently too weak to support much **brand stretching** activity.

12 Integrity

(a) **Key influences on ethical conduct**

Introduction

Notions of right and wrong tend to be conditioned by history eg the behaviour of respected leaders and the tenets of the dominant religion. It is possible to discern an ethical climate in a society, which forms part of its **culture and subtle differences between societies**. It has been reported eg that there is concern in Western Europe for the less rigorous attitudes to corrupt practices in business that Eastern European countries may bring with them when they join the EU. In this regard, *The Times* newspaper reported that 'former communist states have been tainted by corruption through bribery and the black market has become a means of survival in over-regulated, centrally planned economies'.

In light of the above, organisations should be seen as part of human society and, like individual people, are subject to rules that govern their conduct towards others. Because **laws** are important but not adequate, **ethical responsibilities** need to embrace the **integrity and ethical conduct** of senior management and others involved in for example, auditing accounts. What should be expected of business practices in society is to avoid questionable practices, respond to the spirit as well as the letter of the law and do what is right, fair and just. Described below are the key influences, both positive and negative, on **ethical conduct**.

Positive ethical influences

Organisations operate within and interact with the political, economic and social framework of wider society. It is both inevitable and proper that they will both influence and be influenced by that wider framework. They should **establish corporate policies** for those issues over which it has direct control. Examples of matters that should be covered by policies include: environmental effects; political activity; bribery; equal opportunities; health and safety; labelling and support for cultural activities. All of these should have a positive influence on all employees to act as a guide to acceptable ethical behaviour. However, policies alone will not ensure individuals act with integrity. An example of this was the collapse of Enron in 2002 in the USA where the company only paid lip service to their ethical policies.

Policies to **guide the individual behaviour** are likely to flow from the corporate stance on the matters discussed above. Thus the organisation must decide on the extent to which it considers it appropriate to attempt to influence individual behaviour. Some aspects of such behaviour may be of **strategic importance**, especially when managers can be seen as representing or embodying the organisation's standards. Matters of financial rectitude and equal treatment of minorities are good examples.

By publishing **corporate codes of ethical standards**, it comes into the public domain thus making it very clear to senior management and company auditors what is required of them. These should not be over-prescriptive or over-detailed, since this encourages a legalistic approach to interpretation and a desire to seek loopholes in order to justify previously chosen courses of action. However, if individuals collude for their own personal gain and flout the codes, there will be no hiding place from Governments, pressure groups and publications like the 'Ethical Consumer'.

Negative ethical influences

Personal amorality is likely to exist in any organisation to a greater or lesser extent, quite apart from actively **immoral or illegal behaviour**. Such amorality, or lack of care about right and wrong must inevitably lead to **unethical conduct**. For example, financial pressures could be a major problem. This may take the form of personal financial problems resulting from eg gambling, drug use or simple over-spending. Such problems drive individuals to a range of unethical behaviour, ranging from inflated expense claims to outright fraud.

Financial pressures leading to fraud also exist at the corporate level. External pressure from shareholders or markets to improve profitability can lead to bribery to win contracts and all kinds of creative accounting. For example, it is also a specific threat to auditors, since efforts may be made to undermine their impartiality and objectivity. The methods employed may range from simple friendliness and the provision of agreeable lunches for the auditors on site, to threats to take more lucrative consulting business elsewhere if the audit is not verified.

Under such circumstances, unprincipled demands for improved performance are likely to filter down through the organisation as each level of the hierarchy comes under pressure from the one above.

(b) **Influencing ethical behaviour of organisational members**

Coercion is the fallback position of all systems of behaviour control, including law and ethical codes. If organisations and professions want their people to behave in accordance with a particular set of rules, they must be prepared to enforce them. Professional bodies have a set of law-based procedures for doing just that.

Organisations too, are capable of enforcing their ideas about ethics eg an allegation of unethical behaviour at Boeing in late 2003 led to the dismissal of the head of finance and subsequently to the resignation of Phil Condit, chairman and chief executive.

If a willingness to **enforce policies** exists, **codes of ethics** can have an effect both in organisations and in professions. If breaches of such codes are ignored or condoned, they will be treated with contempt and be worse than useless, since they will demonstrate that senior officers are hypocrites as well as unethical in their behaviour. Senior management therefore has several tasks as set out below.

- **To define and give life to an organisation's defining values**
- **To create an environment that supports ethically sound behaviour**
- **To instil a sense of shared accountability amongst employees**

According to Paine there are two approaches to the management of ethics: compliance-based and integrity-based.

A **compliance-based approach** is primarily designed to ensure that the company acts within the letter of the law, and that violations are prevented, detected and punished. Some organisations, faced with the legal consequences of unethical behaviour take legal precautions such as mentioned below.

- **Compliance procedures to detect misconduct**
- **Audits of contracts**
- **Systems to protect and encourage 'whistleblowers'**
- **Disciplinary procedures to deal with transgressions**

Corporate compliance is limited in that it relates only to the law, but legal compliance is not an adequate means for addressing the full range of ethical issues that arise every day. This is especially the case in the UK, where voluntary codes of conduct and self-regulation are perhaps more prevalent than in the US. The compliance approach also overemphasises the threat of detection and punishment in order to channel appropriate behaviour.

An **integrity-based approach** treats ethics as an issue of organisation culture. It combines a concern for the law with an emphasis on managerial responsibility for ethical behaviour. **Integrity strategies** strive to define companies' guiding values, aspirations and patterns of thought and conduct. When integrated into the day-to-day operations of an organisation, such strategies can help prevent damaging ethical lapses, while tapping into powerful human impulses for moral thought and action. Such approaches assume that people are social beings with values that can be supported and refined and thus attempt to integrate ethical values into the organisation (or profession) by providing guidance and consultation and by identifying and resolving problems.

13 Hotel Company

Presentation notes on services marketing

Presented by: Matthew James
Audience: Interview Panel
Resources : Slides, Handout

1 **Introduction**

Good morning ladies and gentlemen. Over the next 30 minutes I would like to outline a number of key characteristics of marketing any service and then relate these to the particular task of marketing a hotel. I'll be happy to take questions at the end of the presentation.

2 **Aims of presentation**

- To outline the distinctive characteristics of marketing a hotel service.
- To consider in what ways the marketing mix should be extended when marketing the services of a hotel.

3 **The characteristics of services**

A service is **any activity or benefit that one party can offer to another** which is essentially intangible and does not result in the ownership of anything. Its production may or may not be tied to a physical product eg renting a hotel room. It can't be physically taken away, nor the transaction be touched. This makes it difficult to evaluate before purchase and means that customers do not own the service.

Thus we are forced to ask: How can the hotel manage this intangibility?

Our task is to try and **'tangiblise the service'**. For example, our staff should look professional wearing a hotel uniform and pay attention to personal grooming. The reception should have quality décor and provide communications material of a high quality. The decor in the rooms should be spotless and follow the hotel's overall decorative identity. The food we serve should be of a high standard and offer our guest variety. Along with this there are other service characteristics. For example:

- **Inseparability**

    Services have simultaneous production and consumption that emphasises the importance of the service provider and therefore the role of our contact personnel. The conference organiser and the waiter, in our customers' eyes, is the hotel. Consequently, selection, training and rewarding staff for excellent service quality is very important. The consumption of the service often takes place in the presence of other customers, as in the restaurant, therefore enjoyment is not only dependent on the service provider but other guests as well. It is important to identify and reduce the risk of possible sources of conflict. For example, our restaurant layout should provide reasonable space between tables and smoking areas.

- **Heterogeneity**

    This characteristic can also be referred to as variability, this means that it is very difficult to standardise the service our guests receive. The receptionist may not always be courteous and helpful; the maids may not remember to change all the towels and so on. Due to inseparability a fault such as rudeness cannot be quality checked and corrected between production and consumption. Therefore, this emphasises the need for rigorous selection, training and rewarding of staff.

    Evaluation systems should be established which give our customers the opportunity to report on their experiences with our staff. In addition we must ensure that our processes are reliable. For example, the way we book in guests, organise their keys and deal with checking-out. No hotel is perfect, however, it is important for any service delivery failures to be responded to immediately.

- **Perishability**

    Consumption cannot be stored for the future. Once a hotel room is left empty for the night, that potential revenue is lost. This makes occupancy levels very important and it is therefore necessary to match supply with demand. In other words, if our hotel is busy in the week but not at weekends, a key marketing task, is to provide incentives for weekend use. To cater for peak demand we can employ part-time staff and multi-skilled, full time staff. We can also use reservation systems in the restaurant and a beauty salon to smooth out demand and ensure that if our customers have to wait, that comfortable seating in the reception is provided.

- **The extended marketing mix**

    The marketing mix is a set of controllable tools known as the four 'hard' Ps. These are: product, price, place and promotion. What was found to be missing, was, the service element for which an additional three 'soft' Ps were added to the tool kit namely, physical evidence; process and people.

    Physical evidence is used to manage the essentially intangible nature of the hotel service. As previously stated, smart staff, an impressive lobby and interior design for all areas of the hotel is important to establish an appropriate position and signal this to customers. **Managing processes** can help to deal with the inseparability and heterogeneity characteristics. If standards and processes are adhered to, a consistent level of service can be delivered eg receptionists need to be trained to deal with demanding business people particularly ensuring that the booking process is both effective and efficient.

    Probably the most important element of the services marketing mix is **people.** As all hotel staff occupy a key position in influencing customer perceptions of service quality, without training and control, staff tend to be variable in their performance. This in turn leads to variable service quality and customer satisfaction.

4 Conclusions

In conclusion, I draw your attention to the advice of key academics in the field of services marketing, such as Bateson, Zeithamal and Bitner, all of whom recommend that there are three key issues for service marketers. These are:

- **Managing differentiation**
- **Managing productivity**
- **Managing service quality**

And finally ... should I be successful in my application today, I too would make these three issues my top priority for the hotel.

Does anybody have any questions?

14 Crisis Management

To: The Board of Directors
From: Penelope Peasgood, PRO
Subject: Crisis Management
Date: 2 May 20X7

1.0 Introduction

Crisis management involves the effective management of communications between our Company and its various **publics** concerning any future crisis. Apart from the devastation caused through terrorism, as was the case on September 11th, crisis can occur as a result of accidents or an act of God. It may also arise as a result of negligence or criminal behaviour by an individual within or outside the organisation. The key to survive is being well prepared for the event and well disciplined once the crisis has developed.

2.0 Preparation

This can be done through **scenario planning** which involves employees meeting together, from different parts and levels of the organisation in order to bring as much experience as possible to the planning table. By **sharing information**, a lengthy list of scenarios of 'what if?' questions can be compiled. These may consist of the likelihood of: an aircraft crashing into the premises; fire in the building; a serious accident on site; in the event of disaster and senior management are not available, etc. Having identified scenarios, individuals within the organisation would be identified as leaders to join a crisis management team with clear responsibilities given at both the planning stage and the time of crisis. The crisis team should include the CEO or his representative; Estates Director; Public Relations Officer; Finance Director; Human Resource Director and other identified individuals. As the PRO I can help to facilitate the proceedings.

3.0 Procedure

Once the crisis management plan has been formulated, the only way to test it is to rehearse. It is too late to practice when the crisis happens. Harrison suggests the following as principles of crisis public relations management:

- **Be prepared** – By rehearsing and meeting regularly (even when the crisis plan has been drawn up) to continually review and update particularly in light of personnel changes and changes in media contacts.

- **Provide background information** – When a crisis happens everything takes place very fast. A multitude of media personnel will descend all wanting their story. If they go away empty handed, a story will come from somewhere to fill the column inches or broadcast minutes. This can often be from unreliable sources. If the PRO has sufficient usable background information, this will help fill the gap by being able to give essential facts and figures, dates, names, photographs, etc. This affords time for the PRO and senior management to gather relevant information to prepare a positive statement.

- **Manage information flow** – In crisis situations it is vital that the organisation takes immediate control of the information process. It is important that the organisation speaks with one voice because the media, stakeholders and general public will be sensitive to any inconsistencies. A well organised, rehearsed and updated crisis management team and internal communication system should manage the flow of information, having first identified the employees who would speak on such issues.

- **Agree the ground rules** – Forward planning should enable the organisation to identify other parties that may share an interest in any crisis that might affect it eg insurers, legal advisers, suppliers, emergency services, etc. Agreement should be obtained beforehand to a set of ground rules of what can and cannot be said publicly without reference to the organisation ie prevention of spokespeople getting in each others way or 'passing the buck' or blaming each other.

- **Be authoritative** – By taking the initiative from the very beginning it is possible to establish the organisation as the authoritative source of information about what has happened and what the organisation is doing about it.

- **Keep talking** – To the media and stakeholders, silence rightly or wrongly indicates something to hide. Continuously talking and providing background information feeds journalists with information they need to take away. It is imperative when unable to offer specific information, to explain that information cannot be offered eg for legal reasons.

- **Say you are sorry** – Cautious lawyers or insurers may advise against saying you are sorry but there is a view that expressing regret is a different matter from making an apology, and that expressing sorrow at a disaster or tragic event is proper behaviour.

- **Ensure accuracy** – It is advisable to ensure that information released by the organisation is truthful and to make sure what is printed in the media is accurate. Serious misrepresentations can be dealt with eg through a letter the Editor, Press Complaints Commission, Lawyers, etc.

- **Be sensitive** – The use of language and appropriateness of style or design of public relations messages need to be sensitive to needs of their publics eg the organisation's shareholders or employees.

- **Learn from experience** – After the crisis, the team can use the experience it has gained to enable the organisation to better prepare for the event of further crisis. By keeping a log of events as they unfold during and after the crisis and by proper de-briefing for all concerned, conclusions can be drawn and lessons learned.

4.0 Conclusion

Business in the 21ˢᵗ Century is so highly competitive and operates with a large degree of unpredictability. In light of this, it is deemed essential to be well prepared for any eventuality to sustain the organisation and its brand's good reputation. Therefore, it is essential that there is a contingency plan and set of procedures to maintain the market position and not succumb to negative publicity in the event of a crisis.

I trust this report fulfils the brief and information contained herein is informative for the Board of Directors.

15 Relationship marketing and IT technology

Introduction

Gummesson states that **'relationship marketing is marketing, seen as a relationship, networks and interaction'.** These relationships require at least two parties who are in contact with each other. The basic relationship of marketing therefore, is between a supplier and a customer. The customer is central to **marketing orientation** but many suppliers sell to intermediaries rather than just to the end consumer. Some sell to both categories and have to recognise that the intermediary (eg manufacturers who maintain their own sales force but appoint agents in remote geographical areas) who sells their products is just as much a customer as the eventual consumer. While it is reasonable to give the highest priority to the needs of the ultimate consumer, an organisation can insist on some control on activities of the intermediary. However, it must be recognised also that agents will only perform well if their own needs are addressed.

Understanding relationship marketing

Adcock argues that relationship marketing can only exist when the marketing function fosters a customer-orientated **service culture** (that reflects attitudes and assumptions). This supports the network of activities that deliver value to the customer. With the emphasis on the long-term nature of commitment and mutual respect, which is sometimes referred to as **marriage**. However, as the knowledge of relationship marketing has developed, there is an understanding that a broader view of 'markets' must be addressed in order to optimise customer relationships. This is highlighted in Christopher *et al's Six-Market Model* shown below.

The Six Market Model

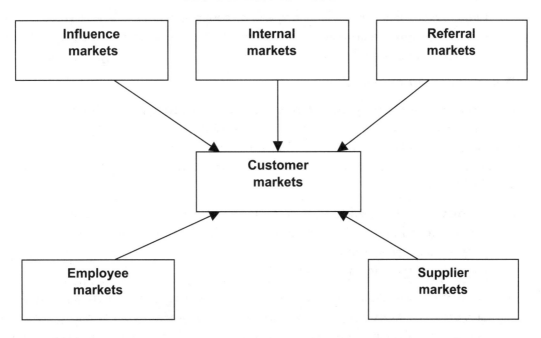

Christopher et al. 1994

Drummond and Ensor suggest that undoubtedly, the customer market should be the primary focus of any organisation and outlines the following.

- **Customer markets**

    The express aim should be to move customers up the marketing **loyalty ladder**. Therefore, the aim is to move from first 'customer catching' = Prospect to Customer – to customer keeping = Client >Support>Advocate, through an emphasis on developing and enhancing relationships.

- **Supplier markets**

    Strong supply links and joint innovation enable the overall supply chain to be optimised. This reduces costs and potentially enhances the quality of the customer experience.

- **Employee markets**

    It is essential to recruit and retain the right employees as ultimately they affect the desired levels of customer satisfaction.

- **Internal markets**

    By treating employees, departments or functions as customers, internal services can be delivered and supported more effectively. This can also assist in motivating employees, improving effectiveness and ultimately enhancing the external customer experience through the use of marketing principles ie the internal marketing mix.

- **Influence markets**

    External groups have a significant influence on the organisation. Therefore, management needs to build relationships with the media, local communities, campaign groups etc. The aim is to maintain the corporate image and facilitate growth of the organisation.

- **Referral markets**

    Organisations that deliver high degrees of customer service are well placed to receive customer referrals from individuals, distributors, trade groups etc. The aim is to strive to establish a wide referral network.

IT in developing relationships

Relationship marketing, **direct marketing** and **data base marketing** ('one-to-one' marketing) are evolving to create a powerful new marketing paradigm through the use of new technology. Information can be made readily available to conduct a unique dialogue between a company and individuals or groups with similar needs. Below is a selection of tools to help support the relationship.

- **Databases** – Are used to store vast amounts of information on customers, suppliers and other interested parties. This can be used to help segment the market into small groups of people with similar interests and needs, enabling a unique message to be sent to that targeted audience via eg direct mail or e-mail.

- **Website** – This allows direct access for all stakeholders, is ideal to capture information and data and to help maintain the marketing relationship. The site allows for one-to-one interaction. This can include eg downloading a brochure; purchasing goods or services; new product information and price changes and, customer support.

- **Intranet** – Allows for up-to-date information to be available to all employees within the organisation and provides the opportunity to interact through eg e-mails, feedback questionnaires and training.

- **Extranet** – This provides an interactive website with limited access to specific channel members and other external parties. It can be used for new product information, price changes and ordering eg Wal-mart allows limited access to their suppliers to check stock levels within stores. It is the supplier's responsibility to maintain stock levels so that Walmart can meet their customer needs.

Conclusion

In today's highly competitive business environment, a way of maintaining **competitive advantage** is to develop and support a relationship with customers, employees and suppliers. As IT has the ability to be instantly updated, it can support all stakeholders, provide a personalised service and build effective long-term relationships.

16 Measuring the value of brands

To: Board of Directors, Springbok Foods
From: Neil Spratt, Brand Manager
Subject: Measuring the Value of Brands
Date: 20th June 20X3

1.0 Introduction

As the Board are aware, creating a successful brand can be very expensive in money, time and effort. When making a significant investment in creating and enhancing a brand, it is appropriate to measure the degree of success that it achieves. During the process of **brand valuation**, it is important to distinguish between **brand *value*** and **brand *values.*** Brand *values* are the intangible factors that make up the identity or image of the brand eg descriptions such as young; active; fun; secure and safe. Brand *value* on the other hand, is value in the economic sense ie the monetary worth of the brand or the cash value it represents.

2.0 Brand value

The valuation of brands is an important aspect of the application of shareholder value analysis to marketing management. Shareholders rightly expect to see a return on their investment. The greater the value achieved from a given cash investment, the better the performance of the organisation and its management is assessed to be. This applies as much to investment in intangible's eg brands, as to investment in tangible ones eg machinery or premises. The problem is that intangible assets are much more difficult to value than tangible ones.

3.0 Methods of valuing brands

There are several methods of calculating brand value, for example:–

- **Cost** – The past costs incurred in building the brand are indexed to current values and summed.
- **Royalties** – Allow for the use of experience in current market conditions.
- **Market value** – Recent sales of comparable brands may be used as a guide to value.
- **Economic use value** – Extra profits attributable to the ownership of the brand are averaged over, say, the last three years and multiplied by, say, 10.

However, *Doyle* dismisses all of these because:

(a) The problem with using historical cost is that its relevance to current value can be extremely limited. This applies to all assets, tangible and intangible.

(b) Calculating the brand value through royalties is no more than guesswork as it is done in the absence of plentiful hard data on actual current royalty rates.

(c) It is difficult to arrive at a market value for tangible assets, as there is a problem with analysing out the values of the individual intangible assets. For example, there may be other intangibles such as established dealer relationships.

(d) While economic use value is seen as a popular method as it can be used to compare brands, the choice of multiple is highly subjective and past performance is a poor guide to the future.

In light of the above, Doyle proposes that brands should be valued by the standard shareholder value approach (SVA) on the basis of the **extra value they will create**.

The SVA approach to brand valuation

To do this it is necessary to forecast the *extra* future cash flows that are expected to bring over and above what an unbranded product would provide. These sums are then discounted to a present value which is the value represented by ownership of the brand. As with all SVA applications, this is subject to the problem that eg SVA depends absolutely on the accuracy with which future cash flows can be forecast and, in particular the **risk** created by the difficulty of establishing a suitable **discount rate** and estimating future **earnings**.

Other methods of calculation include the following:

- The *Interbrand* **brand strength index** which is based on the brand's market qualities. The method used is to score the brand on seven attributes eg stability, legal protection and growth. The total score is out of 100 points.

- *Haigh's* **brand beta analysis** is based on the capital asset pricing market analysis model and takes account of four elements of risk.
    - A risk-free return based on government securities.
    - The extra risk associated with investment and shares.
    - A market sector risk adjustment.
    - The brand risk profile.

Conclusion

When the Board considers the valuation of brands, you should be aware of the differences in **philosophy** that exists, particularly between financial and marketing employees. Accountants are cautious and pessimistic by nature, and their role requires them to be **realistic.** Marketing individuals tend to be **optimistic** and not averse to risk taking and will want their brand-building efforts to be recognised. As a result of these two orientations, problems can be created in valuing a brand. Marketers talk in terms of *investment*, while accountants talk in terms of *cost* and would rather write it off against profit.

An important consideration for the Board is that the rules for financial accounting produce an overall value for the organisation that tends to be very different from its **real market value**. The difference is made up of **intangible value** residing in such things as brands and the expertise of employees. This should be accepted as a problem, but accounting rules have not moved very far towards acceptance of brands as balance sheet assets since they are so difficult to value.

17 Shareholder value analysis

Introduction

In the past, marketing managers have tended to pursue purely **marketing objectives** such as: sales growth; market share; customer satisfaction and brand recognition. None of these necessarily translates into increased **shareholder value**. As a result, marketing has suffered from a lack of perceived relevance to true business value. An emphasis on profitability as a measure of success has led to a certain amount of 'short-termism' in strategic management, with an emphasis on containing and reducing current costs in order to boost current profits. Unfortunately, this approach tends to under-estimate the longer-term affect of such action and can lead to **corporate decline**. Investment in intangible assets eg brands can make a positive contribution to long-term shareholder value.

Shareholder value analysis

This concept is of particular importance to marketing management because their role is generally concerned with activities that create long-term value which are not recognised by traditional accounting-based performance measures. For example, the tangible assets of a small local newspaper may remain constant over a period of say five years. However, the newspaper title ie the brand, may have grown in stature and be able to command a far higher price based on the goodwill built up over that period.

Shareholder value analysis (SVA) is generally carried out by independent Financial Analysts who measure the **value offered by an organisation's shares**. It is a method of approaching the problem of business control by focusing on the creation of value for shareholders, the **company prospects** for generating both cash and capital growth in the future and the **market value** of all the shares in existence (the market capitalisation). If the current market capitalisation is less than the actual value, then the shares are under valued. Investment is therefore necessary to produce either assets that grow in value or actual cash surpluses. In other words, SVA is essentially one of estimating the likely effectiveness of the organisation's **current investment decisions**. Thus, it is both a system for judging the worth of current investment proposals and for judging the performance of the managers who are responsible for the organisation's performance.

Doyle recommends that when considering the total value of a business, it is also necessary to consider the probable residual value of the business in the more distant future. Looking outside the normal planning horizon, he suggests is five years. This assumes no special competitive advantage from current investments and simply uses the cost of capital as an estimate of future earnings.

Value-based management

Doyle suggests that business success should be measured by SVA because of the property rights of shareholders and the pressure to oust management that does not deliver returns. As already stated, marketing objectives are no longer acceptable to investors or the analysts and should be based on what he calls **value based management**. This is:

- A **belief** that maximising shareholder returns is the objective of an organisation.
- The **principles** or strategic foundations of value are (i) to target those market segments where profits can be made (ii) to develop competitive advantage that enables both the customer and the organisation to create value.
- The **processes** concern how strategies should be developed, resources allocated and performance measured.

Value-based management means that purely marketing investment proposals will be judged as described above. Marketing managers should justify their spending requests in such terms on the basis that such spending is not a cost burden to be minimised but an investment in intangible assets such as the following four suggested by Doyle.

- Marketing knowledge
- Brands
- Customer loyalty
- Strategic relationships with channel partners.

The obstacle that lies in the approach to marketing's use of SVA, is the common perception that marketing spending is merely a cost to be controlled and minimised. The onus on marketing managers is to demonstrate that their budgets do in fact create assets, provide competitive advantage for the organisation and that the benefits exceed the costs.

Management should be aware that **SVA has its limitations.** However, it goes some way in developing true business value for the intangible aspects of marketing.

18 Brand strategies and equity

To: Frans Kemper, Marketing Director
From: Sheila Alcock, Brand Manager
Subject: Brand Strategies and Equity
Date: 23rd July 20X6

1.0 Introduction

Murphy suggests a **brand is a simple thing** and in effect, it is a trademark that through careful management, skilful promotion and wide use, appears in the minds of consumers to embrace a particular set of values and attributes both **tangible and intangible**.

2.0 Branding strategies

A number of options are highlighted below.

- **Company** – The company name is the most prominent feature of the brand eg Mercedes.

- **Company brand** - Combined with a **product brand** name eg Kellogg's: Corn Flakes, Rice Krispies, this option both legitimises (because of the company name) and individualises (the individual product name) products. This is sometimes known as **source branding**. This is a **relatively cheap** approach and allows for **new names to be introduced quickly**. It is sometimes used as a short-term measure for saving money.

- **Range brand** - Companies often group types of product under different brands. For example, *Sharwoods* is a brand owned by **RHM Foods**. They also offer *pickles, poppadums, sauces* etc under the same brand. Brands restricted to a small range of goods, is known as a **line brand**.

- **Individual name** – Each product has a unique name. *Procteor & Gamble* choose this option with each of their products having different brand names within the same product line, eg *Bold, Tide,* two of their washing powders.

- **Umbrella brands** – These are used to support several products in very different markets. This shares building costs but may weaken brand identity eg *Philip's* wide range of electrical and electronic products.

3.0 Evaluating branding strategies

Brand Strategy	Advantages	Disadvantage
Company and/or umbrella brand name	<ul><li>Economies of scale</li><li>Easy to launch new products under umbrella brand</li><li>Good for internal marketing</li></ul>	<ul><li>Not ideal for segmentation</li><li>Harder to obtain distinct identity</li><li>Risk that failure in one area can damage the brand eg Virgin Trains</li><li>Variable quality</li></ul>
Range brands	<ul><li>Provides opportunity to enter new market segments with new brand range</li></ul>	<ul><li>New product failure may damage brand range</li></ul>
Individual brand name	<ul><li>Facilitates innovation and creative marketing</li><li>Ideal for precise segmentation</li><li>Crowds out competition but offering more choice</li><li>Damage limitation to company's reputation</li></ul>	<ul><li>Can be costly</li><li>Risky</li></ul>

4.0 Brand equity

A well-managed brand is an asset to any organisation and is often referred to as **brand equity**. It is the marketing and financial value associated with a brand's **strength** in the market. Besides patents and trademarks (the actual proprietary **brand assets**), Aaker suggest four major elements can assist in building brand equity. These are outlined below.

- **Brand name awareness** – This leads to brand familiarity and ultimately comfort with the brand. A familiar brand is selected in preference to an unfamiliar brand because the familiar brand often is viewed as reliable and of acceptable quality.

- **Brand loyalty** – This is a valued component of brand equity because it reduces a brand's vulnerability to competitor's actions. It enables organisations to keep existing customers and reduces costs of gaining new customers. For example, it is estimated it costs five times more to acquire a new customer than retaining an existing one. Loyal customers also provide brand visibility and reassurance to potential new customers as well as expecting their brand to be available when and where they shop. In light of this, retailers endeavour to carry the brands known for their strong customer following.

- **Perceived brand quality** – A brand name itself actually stands for a certain level of quality in a customer's mind and is used as a substitute for actual judgement of quality. Perceived high brand quality can help to support a premium price allowing a marketer to avoid severe market competition. This can also translate into brand extensions as the perceived quality will be able to transfer onto the new product or service.

- **Brand associations** – Marketing sometimes links a set of associations to a brand. These can include lifestyle or a particular personality type. For example, De Beers (a diamond is forever) is associated with a loving, long lasting relationship. These associations can attribute significantly to brand equity.

Conclusion

Brand equity represents the value of a brand to an organisation and can help to give a brand the power to capture and maintain a consistent market share. This provides stability to an organisation's sales volume even though it is difficult to measure.

19 Ethics and social responsibility

To: The Managing Director, Watson & Flounders
From: Stephanie Greene
Subject: Ethics and Corporate Social Responsibility
Date: 26th August 20X0

1 **Introduction**

In 2000, Anita Roddick, Founder of the Body Shop claimed that one of their greatest frustrations was being judged by the media and the City by their profits and not by their principles. The Body Shop is part of a growing band of organisations that now adopt a more ethical and social stance. In particular, in the latter part of the 20th Century, political events, technological invention and sociological events have given rise to the **'ethical consumer'**. Palmer suggests because of the expanding media availability and increasingly **intelligent audience**, it is easier to expose examples of unethical business practice. Many television audiences appear to enjoy watching programmes that reveal alleged unethical practices of household name companies.

2 **Ethics**

Ethics are concerned with a set of moral principles and values that act to a guide of an individual's conduct. *Henderson* suggests there are four positions that an organisation can adopt towards this issue.

- **Ethical and legal** – It is ideal that decisions are both legal and ethical eg the Body Shop claim to be this.

- **Unethical and legal** – Decisions require a trade-off of ethics for legality eg gazumping.

- **Ethical and illegal** – Decisions require a trade-off of legality in favour of ethical choice eg publishing stolen but revealing documents about government mismanagement.

- **Unethical and illegal** – Decisions both illegal and unethical should be avoided eg employing child labour.

When marketing managers are operating internationally eg in Africa, **bribes** to conduct business are a **standard practice**. Managers have to decide whether to conform with local expectations or adhere to home country values. This can create a **dilemma** of either increasing company profits or sticking rigidly to your ethical stance.

3 **Corporate social responsibility**

This about the organisation accepting that it is part of society and as such will be accountable to that society for the consequences of the actions which it takes. This is different from ethics in that it comes under three headings:

- Consumer issues
- Community relations
- Green marketing

Organisations may not implement all three, however, the Body Shop for example, regards all three as vital to their success.

4 **Building ethics and social responsibility into the business**

Having discussed the above, there is a need to build ethics into the framework of the organisation. A way of doing this is to use marketing activities eg **the marketing mix** to implement them.

- **Ethical issues relating to products** – Care must be taken to ensure the consumer of **safety**, **quality** and **value** and adequate **information** provided. In other words, if a fault is identified with a **product**, then it needs to be immediately **recalled**. For example, *Perrier* immediately withdrew all supplies when they discovered their water was contaminated. Even though they suffered losses, their reputation was enhanced.

- **Ethical issues relating to promotions** – **Promotional practices** such as advertising and personal selling are areas in which the temptation to select, exaggerate, slant, conceal and distort information is potentially very great. Questionable practices such as this are likely to create **cynicism in the customer** and ultimately to preclude any degree of trust or respect. Therefore, it is important that in all promotional activities, they **must be legal, decent, honest and truthful**.

Answer Bank

- **Ethical issues relating to pricing** – Active collusion among suppliers to fix prices is illegal in most countries. **Predatory pricing** allows established suppliers to utilise their cash reserves and economies of scale to sell at prices way below that of new comers into the market. This can drive newcomers out of the market. There may be a short-term gain to this, but unethical practice on pricing could ultimately be the organisation's downfall.

- **Ethical issues relating to place** – Where long and complex distribution channels are used, there is potential for disputes and conflicts of interest. These could include:
    - Manipulating discount structures to the detriment of distributors
    - Ending distribution agreements at short notice
    - Dealing direct with end users.

    All of the conduct above could break long established relationships originally built on trust over long periods of time. Therefore, regular and constant two-way communication ethically conducted can avoid this taking place.

5 **Ethical codes**

It is now common for organisations to specify their ethical standards. Some even publish a formal declaration of their principles of rules and conduct. It is therefore recommended that your organisation consider a similar approach.

6 **Conclusion**

Today it is considered an astute purchasing decision for consumers to reward only those businesses that have a good record for making quality products, honour guarantees, exchange faulty goods and provide good after-sales service, etc. *Palmer* suggests, in market sectors that are dominated by similar product offers, an ethical position may give a business a **competitive advantage** in the eyes of some customer segments.

20 Service quality

To: Carlos Ferreira, CEO, Realto Hotels
From: Luigi Mennoti, Customer Relations Manager
Subject: Service Quality
Date: 16th April 20X3

1.0 **Introduction**

Service quality is a significant factor that customers use for differentiating between competing services and **can only be defined by customers**. In our industry, with the increase in customer expectations and the effects of consumerism, it is important that there is a high quality of service and that we aim to get it right first time. The strategic approach should be to close the gap between customer expectations and their experiences. As customer perception is formed in a matter of seconds of a service encounter, we only have a very limited time to make an impression.

2.0 **'Moments of Truth'**

The former CEO of SAS Airline calls these service encounters '**moments of truth**'. This can make the difference between success and failure thus, it is crucial to convince our customers that we are the best alternative for their needs. However, the **inseparability** of the service (which means that the services are produced at the same time as they are consumed) makes it difficult to standardise and control the service. Therefore, our service quality should be such that we positively influence the customer's perception so that we are their preferred choice when making a future hotel reservation.

3.0 Delivering service quality

Providing high quality service on a consistent basis is very difficult. However, measures can be taken to increase the likelihood of provision of high quality service. Using the Model: *A Conceptual Model of Service Quality* which is an adaptation of the famous 'SERVQUAL' model devised by *Parasuraman, Zeithaml and Berry* (as shown below), gaps can be identified and hurdles overcome.

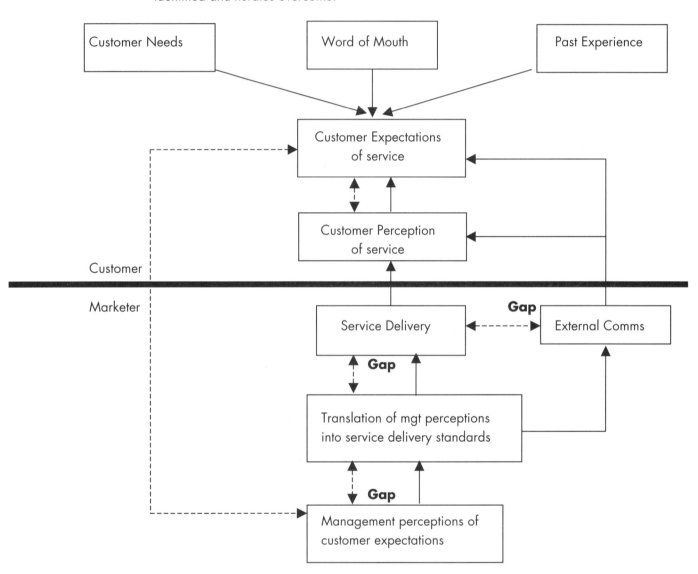

A Conceptual Model of Service Quality and its Implications

This model shows the problems that can occur in the delivery of a service as there are a number of gaps in terms of customer perceptions, expectations and management expectations and perceptions.

4.0 The Identification of Gaps

It is important that the gaps are identified.

- The gap between management perception and customer exceptions will illustrate that the management may not appreciate the customers' needs

- The gap between service quality specifications and management perception – which means that the management does not set standards of performance
- The gap between service quality specification and the delivery of service – which means that operational personnel may be inadequately trained to meet the standards required
- The gap between service delivery and external communications – where the expectations from the promotional activity are not matched in practice
- The gap between perceived and expected service – where customers envisage a better service than the one that has been provided.

Customer care is about ensuring that a service is well managed and that Board level management is committed to improving quality, performing at high standards and implementing a system for monitoring the level of service performance. Within our sector, customer care is critical because people are looking for a 'home from home' and therefore, it is important that they feel comfortable in their surroundings. If not, they will not return and could promote negative word of mouth.

5.0 New Customer Care Programme

It is important to implement Total Quality Management (TQM) within the organisation. This aims to ensure quality practices throughout all processes and relationships within the hotel group.

There are three guiding principles to TQM as follows:

- Recognising the importance of the guest
- Developing 'win-win' relationships with the guest (ie moving their room to a higher specification if they have a complaint)
- Developing trust with the guest

To introduce a customer care programme we will need to take the following steps:

5.1 **Analyse our current procedures** – we need to know what we are doing at present and what guests want. This means actually doing some research. This may require some observation of the staff and customer questionnaires.

5.2 **Develop Service Standards** - after we have found out what we are doing at the moment, and what our customers want, we can develop some service standards. This will give our staff guidelines to ensure that they achieve the correct standard.

5.3 **Set up Systems for Service Delivery** – ensure that systems are put into place to ensure optimum delivery of service. Ie new computer system to allow quicker checkins.

5.4 **Analysis of Staff Training Needs** – Find out what our staff need to be trained on ie should our room service staff be trained in food hygiene or the reception staff go on a customer care course?

5.5 **Introduce Staff Training** – ensure that all training requirements are met. We cannot expect our staff to deliver good service if they are not trained to do so.

5.6 **Set up Monitoring and Measurement Systems** – this will allow us to check that service delivery meets our standards. This will keep staff on their toes and may identify areas for further training. This could be done using a 'mystery guest' programme on a regular basis.

5.7 **Introduce Performance Related Pay and Reward Schemes** – this recognises the staff who do well and rewards them, it may also incentives poorer performing staff to try harder.

6.0 **Conclusion**

I trust the above meets with your requirements. The importance of service quality within our industry has been demonstrated and it is believed the proposed customer care programme would fit the structure of the organisation and therefore allow for easy implementation.

21 Push and Pull

> *Examiner's comment.* A contrast between push and pull should be made in part (a), and part (b) should emphasise the importance of key account management and long-term support.

(a) There are three strategies that can be used by this company when launching a new range. They can be used independently, or together, depending upon the resources available, the target audiences, the objectives set, the competition and the present reputation of the company.

   (i) **Push**- to influence the distributor to stock the new range and develop our relationship. They, in turn, will encourage the end user to buy our range at point of sale.

   (ii) **Pull**- Communications aimed at the end consumer so that they be aware of the range and wish to buy.

   (iii) **Profile**- aimed at all relevant stakeholders, including internal audiences, to build company reputation.

   Our company has an established reputation amongst office retailers, but the new range is also appropriate for home office use. Therefore a mix of push and pull strategies should be used.

   Firstly, distributors will be encouraged to take the full range and display it well, and include it in their catalogues and own promotions (push).

   Secondly, a pull strategy aimed at end users (both purchasing managers and home customers) will create awareness, generating demand and store traffic. This will in turn encourage distributors to support the launch.

(b) **Suggested mix to reach channel members**

   (i) **Personal selling** is important in business-to-business relationships since it builds trust. The sales force can demonstrate the product benefits and negotiate discounts and local promotional support. They will also advise on **merchandising** displays and give training.

   (ii) **Point of purchase** material will be made available, stressing the quality of the product, along with literature that can be used by the distributor to mail out to their customers or distribute in store.

   (iii) **Non personal direct marketing**. This might include a secure **extranet** site, so that distributors can get information on stock availability, order status and product specifications. **Direct mail** to launch the range may be used to pre-warn distributors, or initially to tell new retailers about the range, and the special benefits of stocking the range.

(iv) **CD ROMs** could be mailed out to distributors with room design software included, so that distributors can offer this benefit to their customers when selling the new range. The disk will carry the catalogue.

(v) **Sales promotions.** Special discounts for large orders or pre launch discounts will encourage sales into the distributor. Incentives and competitions for distributor sales teams will encourage their support at the point of sale.

(vi) **Exhibitions** supported by corporate hospitality will create interest in the new range and facilitate dialogue between the company and its distribution network.

(vii) **Advertising** in trade journals will create awareness and may encourage opportunities for PR support.

(viii) **Public relations** will feature the new range and tell of the support that will be offered to the distributors on taking the new range.

Conclusion

Support from members of the supply chain is extremely important for a furniture manufacturer such as ours. **Push strategies must be undertaken to encourage dialogue with channel members**, and ensure that they have the right tools to sell on the products. The mix will be used to create awareness, persuade distributors to take stock, develop relationships and create sales. The push strategies must be integrated with pull techniques to ensure long-term success for the new range.

22 RUS plc

(a) **Relevance to TQM**

TQM is more than just a set of techniques. Developed in manufacturing industry, it is an approach to dealing with production that involves getting things right first time ie **zero defects**. It tries to **involve the customer's needs** in the very process of production. This is obviously relevant to service industries, with the proviso that bad service cannot be inspected and scrapped after it is delivered. This is because services are generally consumed as they are produced and the success in a service industry depends on repeat business. Thus getting things right first time (as this could be the only time) must be a priority. Therefore **TQM** is relevant to both the previous and the proposed new strategy for Jacaranda plc.

Denning, one of the foremost influential proponents of **TQM**, argues: why repeat mistakes? His opinion being that every hotel built, for example, should be an improvement from the previous one. He also suggests that **TQM** is comprised of two strands.

(i) **Quality of design** - In terms of service, the question should always be: Does it meet customer needs in the most appropriate way?

(ii) **Quality of conformity to design** - Does the service delivered actually conform to the service promised?

TQM also involves a detailed analysis of the process of production. An aspect of TQM is the reduction in variation eg restaurant service should be predictable and food quality must be consistently good.

The culture of TQM also must be considered. Staff must be encouraged to come forward with suggestions, and they must be engaged in the process of improving service. There is no reason why these considerations should not apply to the family and medium-priced business accommodation as well as to the hotels new strategy. However, as guests will be paying more, their expectations will be so much higher. The design quality of the service (what these new customers actually want) is therefore paramount, and conformance quality must be faultless. As the **new positioning strategy** of providing a high quality service for the discerning guest may bring fewer customers, their repeat business will be even more valuable.

(b) **Financial and organisational implications**

Jacaranda plc is aiming at a different market, targeting high spending customers whose requirements will be different from the previous target market. This will create financial and organisational implications as well as a need for **further investment** in buildings and fixtures as listed below.

- Decoration
- Changes to room sizes (**eg conversion of pairs of single rooms into suites**)
- More luxurious furnishings
- Perhaps expanded restaurant and kitchen facilities
- Swimming pool, gymnasium etc
- More opulent public spaces

Other expenditure will include:

- More staff, to provide the service required
- More training
- The greater variety of food offered to guests (hence kitchen costs will rise)
- Advertising to reach the target segment

In the past, Jacaranda plc catered for family and business customers at different times. The new strategy requires the same type and standard of service to be maintained at all times. Thus more effort will need to be spent on management, marketing and quality circles should be introduced.

The new approach should also include **training of existing and new staff**. All **staff should be encouraged to participate** in improvement of service management via a **'suggestion box'**. The incentive for this could be, that for all suggestions implemented, individuals responsible will be rewarded. Training will ensure that all staff will develop their skills and be professionally more capable of catering for the new client group.

Overall, from a business perspective, while the new strategy includes training and financial investment and is both time consuming and expensive, in the long term, it will prove **cost effective** as the new customers will be paying much more per head.

23 Great Utility Services Ltd

(a) **Project management**

A project is an endeavour to accomplish a specific objective through a unique set of interrelated tasks and the effective utilisation of resources. It has a **specific timeframe** or **finite life span**. It has a start time and a date by which the objective must be accomplished. In this case the introduction of a new system. Therefore, project management is not directed at maintaining or improving a continuous activity but to its end.

According to *Lock*, all projects involve the projection of ideas and activities into new endeavours and no two projects can ever be the same. The steps and tasks leading to completion can never be described accurately in advance and there can be. Therefore according to Lock, 'the job of project management is to foresee as many dangers as possible and to plan, **organise and control activities** so that they are avoided.'

Managing a project involves **overseeing a team of people** assembled to carry out the work and who must be able to **communicate effectively** and immediately with each other. There can be many unexpected problems working at the limits of existing and new technologies, each one of which should be resolved by careful design and planning prior to commencement of work. There should be mechanisms within the project to enable these problems to be resolved during the time span of the project without detriment to the objective, the cost or the time span.

There is normally no benefit until the work is completed. The **'lead in' time** to this can cause a strain on the eventual recipient who feels deprived until the benefit is achieved even though in many cases it is a major improvement on existing activities. Also, contributions made by specialists are of differing importance at each stage. Assembling a team working towards the one objective is made difficult due to the tendency of specialists to regard their contribution as being more important than other people and not understanding the inter-relationship between their various specialities in the context of the project.

Therefore, the project manager should endeavour to **negotiate with all parties** with differing interests in the outcome to ensure the mutual success of the project.

(b) **Techniques and objectives of project management**

Having defined the project, it has an objective that must be achieved. A technique for making this clear is the specification prepared by or with the client. This defines the **scope of the project**. Constantly changing client specifications can increase the cost of the project and lead to its failure.

In order for the project to meet its objectives, quality must be assured through **compliance to client specifications and any appropriate safeguards**. Some information systems methodologies are modelled on previous successes and involve implementation through a series of steps.

To ensure the right level of quality is achieved, a systems project will require **specific documentation** to ensure there have been no short cuts taken. Tests should be carried out and fully documented. For greatest benefit eg the quality controls over the project should relate to British and International standards eg BS 5750 and ISO 9000. This will also give additional assurance to the client.

Budget and timescale can be dealt with together. In order to plan the project effectively, a number of techniques are used. A **work breakdown structure** is the analysis of the work of a project into different units or tasks. It identifies the work that must be done, determines the resources required, sequences the work done, and allocates resources in the optimum way. These can then be mapped on **Gantt charts**, or even on **critical path analysis** to find the optimal allocation of resources to activities. Some activities can be crashed or shortened by throwing more resources at them. However, this could risk increasing the cost of the project. Other activities might be less urgent, depending on the critical path. Therefore, **estimating the timescale** is very important, as for many commercial contracts there are penalties for late completion.

A **standard costing system** might be implemented in that estimates can be prepared, based on the work breakdown structure, and include the resources used by each activity. These estimates may help to minimise risk.

To prevent the risk of a project running late or over budget, the **specification** must be as accurate as possible. To further minimise risk, **insurance** might compensate for some of the immediate financial problems.

In some cases, a project may have to be over-specified with fail-safe mechanisms that can be dealt with by means of contingency plans eg some firms have back-up computer systems if an application is judged to be critical.

(c) **Skills and attributes of a good project manager**

A good project manager will successfully accomplish the objectives to satisfy the client. Therefore, the skills and attributes required of a good project manager include some of the following.

- **Communication** – how he or she communicates to all publics.
- **Problem solving** – be adept with solving a variety of problems along the project schedule by lateral or creative thinking and allocating time to think problems through.
- **Team building** – having the skills to build and motivate the team during the project.
- **Leadership** – ability to adapt leadership styles by recognising that during some situations, they may need to be autocratic while at other times, they will empower people to get on with their task.
- **Negotiations** – the challenge is to find a way of accommodating the various parties involved in the project and emerging with some kind of agreement about the best way of proceeding and moving the process forward.
- **Organisational skills** – if they can't organise, they can't manage. The project has to run to specific deadlines and without exceptional organisational skills, completion of the project would be seriously at risk.

A guideline for a project manager could be summarised in the following rules:

1. Understand the problems, opportunities and expectations of a project manager.
2. Recognise that project teams will have conflicts but these are a natural part of group development.
3. Understand who the stakeholders are and their agendas.
4. Realise that organisations are very political and therefore politics should be used to your advantage.
5. Realise the project management is leader intensive and that he/she must be flexible.
6. Understand that project success is defined by four components: **budget, schedule, performance criteria and customer satisfaction**.
7. Realise that a cohesive team must be built by being a motivator, coach, cheerleader, peacemaker and conflict resolver.
8. Notice that the team will develop attitudes based on the emotions that the project manager exhibits, both positive and negative.

9 Always ask 'what if?' questions and avoid becoming comfortable with the status of the project.

10 Don't get bogged down in minutiae and loose sight of the purpose of the project.

11 Manage time efficiently.

12 Above all plan, plan, plan.

24 Project guide to conferences

Introduction

A project, such as a sales launch conference, is an undertaking that has a defined beginning and end and has resources specifically allocated to it. The intention is to do it only once, and follows a plan towards a clear and intended end-result.

For a project to be successful, two broad ranges of activities – **planning and doing** – are carried out. Within these activities a project moves through stages either, before, during or after the project. These stages are known as the **project life cycle** and are listed below.

- Before the project (definition)
- Before the project (planning)
- During the project (implementing)
- During the project (controlling)
- After the project (completing)

Definition stage

When an opportunity is seen to do something new, this is usually when projects originate. In planning a conference to launch a new product, a decision must be made with regard to the likely business advantages before committing resources to it. In doing so, the **objectives** for the conference are also discussed. For example, the following questions can be asked: Number of potential sales leads? Number of potential orders?; Level of awareness? Along with this it should be decided: What the conference should cover? What suppliers should be used? How much can be spent?

Planning stage

The aim of this stage is to devise a workable scheme to create the conference. Having booked the conference centre, detailed planning will also involve consulting on specific requirements (particularly those for any overseas delegates, confirming the booking of hotel rooms if overnight accommodation is required, arranging audio visual facilities, and confirming catering (including special dietary requirements).

It is imperative to be **client-focused**. In the case of a client from a high technology company, the venue must offer any facilities that they may require, eg IT equipment and Internet facilities. Consideration must be given to the number of delegates attending, as rooms must be neither too big nor too small to accommodate them.

Implementation stage

This stage is concerned with **co-ordinating people** and other resources to actually bring the conference to life. On the day of the conference, organisers, guest speakers and delegates will need to be received. To ensure their comfort, provision should be made for a suitable meeting room on arrival with refreshments etc. In the likely event that some problems may arise on the day, sufficient troubleshooting staff should be on hand to handle the situation.

Controlling stage

This stage is concerned with ensuring that conference objectives are met within the stipulated timeframe, and corrective action is taken where necessary. A specially appointed master of ceremony should lead the conference and venue staff must be liaised with.

Completion stage

The conference project is brought to an orderly end, by asking the following questions:

- Were the facilities satisfactory, and did they perform as promised or expected?
- Were delegates and speakers satisfied with the experience?
- Have feedback questionnaires been issued to participants and completed?
- Are there any outstanding issues, either internally or with the venue?
- Have all outstanding monies been paid?
- Will the conference be repeated next year?
- What can we learn from this for next time?
- Celebrate success!

Evaluation

In the event of failure, reasons need to be identified. Some of which might include the following.

Cause	Action
Lack of appropriate expertise and approach from project leader	Need to focus on development of individual's specific needs to ensure future project success
Lack of financial investment	Seek out sponsor for future events
Lack of ability or necessary expertise of team members	More care to be taken with recruitment, selection and training in order to have the desired individuals with the rights skills to carry out the job

25 Creativity and innovation

To: Josh Doogle, CEO Doogle & McHeggarty Ltd
From: Alison Edwards, Peoples' Partnership
Subject: Creativity and innovation
Date: 20 June 20X9

1.0 Introduction

Creativity can be defined as the ability of the organisation to look at what is done from different perspectives whilst remaining focused on target groups. **Innovation** can be defined as the ability of the organisation to implement new processes and introduce new products and services that generate the right response from target groups.

Michael Porter, a world-renowned business consultant, suggests that creativity leads into innovation and is the central issue in economic prosperity. It has also been said that an organisation is only as good as the people within. In order to assess the capabilities of the organisation to exploit **innovation and creativity** in its products/services and processes, there is a need to develop and nurture the people, processes and techniques within, to ensure economic prosperity.

While it has been identified that there is a need to develop a new culture of creativity and innovation, Doogle & MacHeggarty Ltd should carry out a critical assessment a.k.a. **an**

audit, of the current situation to assess how well they are able to deliver the level and type of innovation necessary to continue to meet and exceed customer needs and expectations.

2.0 Innovation Audit

The innovation audit is a critical assessment of the organisation's innovation record, the internal obstacles to innovation and how performance can be embraced. *Drummond and Ensor* have identified four key areas for this audit:

3.0 The current organisational climate

Doogle & MacHeggarty Ltd will need to overcome barriers to innovation in the form of **resistance to change** from employees and established managers whose aim is to protect their *status quo*. Also, some managers may be ignorant of the new thinking. This can be demonstrated physically by the boss's door being permanently shut. This gives out the message that they are closed to new ideas.

While the traditional business practice may view creativity and innovation as vital, it is not classified as urgent because the bottom line benefits may not be felt for two or three years. **Investment considerations** therefore, are not forthcoming as there is no immediate return.

If senior management have an **autocratic style** with a preference for tight **centralised control** and are not convinced of the benefits of innovation, then innovation will not happen.

4.0 Overcoming barriers

The most effective way of overcoming barriers is through the **commitment of top management**. The CEO in particular needs to be convinced of the appropriateness of the new thinking and be enthusiastic about its implementation throughout the organisation ie they must 'walk the talk'.

As Doogle & MacHeggarty Ltd is a relatively small but growing business, it may be beneficial to **change the traditional company hierarchy**. This will mean no specific job titles with people working in small multidisciplinary teams, each with the responsibility to develop innovative ideas. By fostering a culture of encouragement of creative thought and risk taking, rather than putting people in 'boxes', could lead to more fulfilled, empowered and motivated individuals offering a source of competitive advantage and ultimately lead to a more successful organisation.

Another way to overcome barriers is to change attitudes. This can be accomplished by **training and development**. The individuals chosen to implement any new programme must be enthusiastic and capable of overcoming resistance to change.

5.0 Measure the current organisational performance with regard to innovation

An important input to innovation is the degree of **customer satisfaction**, both from the product itself and service levels. This can be measured on a scale eg from highly satisfied to highly dissatisfied. Customers can also be asked to identify which features of a service/product they found most useful. Customer satisfaction should **actively measured** rather than for the organisation to simply react to complaints.

The diagram below illustrates performance and importance. Doogle and MacHeggarty Ltd should be most concerned if an audit reveals 'high importance' with ' low performance'. In other words, if a service or product of high importance to a customer is perceived to demonstrate 'high importance - low performance', then innovation may be necessary to move it to the 'high performance - high importance' category.

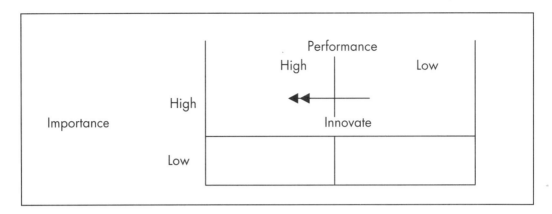

Customer satisfaction rating is not the only means to measuring current performance with regard to innovation. The **balance scorecard** and **innovation/value matrix** could also be used.

6.0 Review of policies and practices

Policies and practices supporting innovation and facilitating it should be reviewed. The objective for management is to create a more outward-looking organisation. Individuals should be encouraged to look for new products, markets, processes and designs and **seek ways to improve productivity**.

Innovation strategy calls for a management policy of **giving encouragement** to innovative ideas, as well as the following:

- Give **financial backing** to innovation, by spending on R&D and market research and risking capital on new ideas.
- Give employees the **opportunity to work** in an environment where the exchange of ideas for innovation can take place.
- **Actively encourage** employees and customers to put forward new ideas.
- **Quality circles** and **sharing information** can be used to encourage creative thinking about work issues.

Where appropriate, **recruitment policy** should be directed towards appointing employees with the necessary skills for doing innovative work.

Along with the traditional change to company hierarchy, an open flow of **two-way communication** is vital to success. Certain individuals should be made responsible for obtaining information outside the organisation about innovative ideas, and for communicating this information throughout the organisation.

Strategic planning should result in targets being set for innovation, and successful achievements by employees should be rewarded.

7.0 The balance of styles of the management team

Even though Doogle and MacHeggarty Ltd is a small organisation, the dynamics of the team affects the corporate culture of the whole organisation. *Belbin* advises that there should be a blend of characteristics to make up an efficient and effective team. In this case, some individuals may have to also adopt their next preferred role to meet the objectives of the organisation. For example, an individual identified as a Co-ordinator may also have to perform as a Team Worker.

Furthermore, leadership style has a direct effect on individuals and teams a like. Only a particular style eg democratic would be most favourable and compatible to foster innovation throughout the organisation. However, to be truly democratic all employees must be willing to participate. There will be times however, when decisions need to be made and it may be necessary to adopt an autocratic style.

26 Creative people

Introduction

Interviewed for an article in *People Management*, Kristina Murrin, co-author of *'Sticky Wisdom'*, suggests **creativity is largely in the hands of the individual** and that it is the characteristics of: freshness, greenhousing, realness, momentum, signalling and courage, that make creative people stand out from the rest. Research has found that creative thinkers are not necessarily born 'different' to anyone else, but through practice and encouragement – first by parents and teachers and then employers – it can be developed. To understand the implications in the work context and what is meant by each characteristic, Murrin offers the following.

Freshness

This can be defined as: doing something different and seeking new stimuli. Commodities are becoming the order of the day and fewer products and services offer differentiation. To combat this, Unilever Best Foods, for example, introduced two programmes with the intention of stimulating and adding freshness to their organisation.

The first, known as the 'germination process' involved individuals being nominated from every team to become 'stimuli hunters'. Their role was to spend time outside the workplace to observe and search for new stimuli. On return, their objective was to 'plant a seed' to germinate a new way of thinking and move the team into new directions. The other programme was 'feel the pulse'. 1,500 managers left their factory, laboratory or office for three days twice a year to visit consumers in their homes and learn more about them. This enables Unilever to continuously keep their finger on the 'pulse' (needs and wants) of their consumers.

Greenhousing

It is not likely for creativity and innovation to come in a sudden flash of inspiration and lead to the invention and perfection of a solution. While new ideas are vital to the survival of business, it takes time to perfect them and without protection for them in a business environment that seeks immediate benefits, they can be brushed aside or crushed by daily tasks. Therefore, there is a need to 'greenhouse' (protect) young ideas when they are at their most vulnerable.

Breaking free from a traditional robust male culture where sarcasm was the norm, Six Continents (formerly Bass) brewing company, adopted a football analogy for individuals who trample on ideas in meetings. For an offender's first offence, they are issued with a yellow card. A second offence or a particularly negative comment receives a red card, and the individual responsible is asked to leave the meeting. While the system is implemented in a playful manner, the intent is serious.

Realness

This refers to the ability to keep in touch with the real world and turn ideas into reality ie it is about getting close to customers and asking how to make good ideas work, rather than toss them into a vacuum. To do this, an organisation could produce a prototype of the product or service they want to develop ie turn thoughts into something real and ask them what they think.

Saatchi & Saatchi, for example, when it was pitching for British Rail business, kept senior rail officials waiting in a dirty ashtray filled room until their patience almost ran out and they were about to leave. At this point, the Saatchi team entered and explained that this was how British Rail's customers felt they were treated. To this end, they then presented advertising that sought to address this frustration. Needless to say, they won the account with their creativity and risky style.

Momentum

This is about making things happen. Successful 'ideas people' suggest the art of maintaining momentum is to say no to pointless activities. For example, to prevent duplication and save valuable time, they question whether they are they really needed at a meeting? They will focus on keeping things moving by questioning what the worst outcome of their ideas could be. The aim is to be proactive ie creating a crisis is a short-term strategy for producing momentum, but the long-term solution is aligning personal and organisational objectives.

A good example of this is, the CEO of Apple rationalised their many diverse projects underway and focused on the professional and the home computer user only and on the desktop and mobile hardware only. His view was that time wise, decisions could be turned around in hours rather than weeks and senior management could get much more involved in the details of ideas.

Signalling

This involves communicating changes of direction to colleagues instead of expecting them to be mind-readers. This helps individuals navigate in a judgement-free world where ideas are allowed to grow. Signalling can help colleagues decide how best to respond to creative ideas – whether you want them to judge an idea or help with building it into something bigger and better.

An example to illustrate this was the actions of a former Asda director, who had a kitchen built in the middle of the marketing department at Head Office. His intention was to remind his employees that the focus of the business is food. Microsoft is another example where they refer to headquarters as a 'campus'. This shows how they company value the nurturing of ideas.

Courage

This involves the creative personality or organisation having the courage to stand up and be counted. Inhibition often results in the loss of great ideas. While it is human nature to stick to what feels safe and not expose ones self to emotional risk, there is a need for individuals to step out of their comfort zone and confront their own fears. This can do wonders for personal development.

Managers themselves need the courage to push for the best performance in others and not accept second best. This would entail more work for both individual and manager. If management takes the easy option, this may result in regret. Therefore, real courage is about forcing change and having to face up to becoming popular.

Conclusion

Most creative teams are drawn from individuals from diverse backgrounds who have a wide spread of knowledge and skills. If individuals are managed well, they will come up with creative solutions, share information, trust each other and be committed to serving the customer. However, if they are not well managed, they can become involved in conflict and more concerned with who wins an argument rather than focussing on the task at hand. Employers need to realise that people who are too busy hitting deadlines and getting jobs done, are being starved of creative expression when they need intellectual space to allow them to develop.

Answer Bank

27 Outsourcing marketing activity

> *Tutorial note.* No format is specified for this question. You may choose to present it as a report or memo, or as raw content such as you might compile for your own reference, to prepare for a meeting on the subject. Note the mention of the strong branding of your organisation: this will be an important factor in outsourcing decisions.

(a) **Identifying the marketing skills required over the next three years**

The demand for marketing skills can be identified by examining:

(i) The organisation's objectives (with reference to the five year plan). The demand for marketing skills will depend on proposed levels of activity in areas such as new product launches, brand reinforcement, target increase in market share, diversification of the brand range, new marketing avenues and technologies (for example, on-line marketing)

(ii) Environmental factors: trends in technology and markets that will require additional marketing skills (eg the explosive growth of e-commerce and the need to have a Web presence to match the strength of our brand) or fewer marketing skills (eg the automation of customer relationship management functions, on-line customer feedback gathering and so on)

(iii) Likely competitor activity: where intelligence can be gathered, it may indicate avenues and extent of marketing skills required to compete effectively

(iv) Benchmark organisations: what marketing skills are being sourced (and outsourced) by key players in our industry.

Given that marketing is a discipline in which forecasts are quickly rendered obsolete by change and uncertainty, a short-term strategic model of HR planning may be most suitable. We could adopt a key issues orientation: HR and marketing managers collaborate to determine what the key issues for human resourcing will be – including (for example) flexibility (speed of response to emerging threats and opportunities) and e-marketing expertise.

(b) **Reasons for and against outsourcing of marketing activities**

Advantages of outsourcing marketing activities

(i) Outsourcing reduces labour and associated costs of carrying out the activities in-house.

(ii) If the subcontractor is well-chosen, outsourcing can give access to specialist skills, knowledge, experience and network contacts in relevant fields, which may be lacking within the organisation.

(iii) Outsourcing takes advantage of contractors' potentially wide experience in different industry contexts: potential for benchmarking, cross-over of techniques from other sectors, seeing the bigger picture which in-house marketers may not be able to provide.

(iv) Contractors may offer objectivity on current marketing strategies, where internal management cannot.

Disadvantages of outsourcing marketing activities

(i) Fees/commissions and the costs of in-house management/liaison to control projects may be high.

(ii) Subcontractors may lack awareness of our organisation culture and values and brand attributes. This will take time to brief in, and will require detailed monitoring and control of all outsourced activities: the strength of our brand must be protected by consistency of the marketing message. Change (if appropriate) must be gradual and sensitive to existing brand perceptions.

(iii) There may be insufficient accountability for results, compared to in-house managerial accountabilities.

(iv) Outsourcing activities which are currently conducted in-house will result in redundancies or transfers, which may damage staff morale and (unless carefully handled) our employer brand in the textile industry.

(c) **Identifying activities for outsourcing or retaining in-house**

The required marketing skills identified in the initial forecast (outlined in (a) above) should be compared to a detailed skills audit of the existing marketing function, taking into account the potential for development of existing staff and the costs of developing or recruiting required skills from the external labour pool) over the same three year period. Any outsourcing proposals will have to be subjected to detailed cost-benefit analysis.

However, some general thoughts on what may be outsourced and retained are as follows.

Outsource	Retain
Advertising: ■ media buying ■ campaign development ■ creative services and production co-ordination	Marketing strategy: while we can take advice from consultants, the strength of our brand requires central control over its direction
Below the line/public relations: ■ media relations ■ corporate PR/financial relations ■ sponsorship ■ events planning ■ crisis management	Trade promotions and public relations: eg exhibitions, trade fairs, conferences. (Our contacts here are likely to be better than agencies – and will benefit from continuity.)
Market research	Marketing management: all marketing activity should be planned, co-ordinated and controlled in house, to ensure accountability and integration
Website and e-commerce development (outside our current expertise)	Brand identity: until and unless we decide to alter our brand and require objective and expert help to manage the change

28 Innovation

Introduction

With reference to the statement 'Innovation is often referred to as the 'life blood' of an organisation', fierce competitive global market developments and a technological revolution have led to **shorter product life cycles**. Therefore, the only way to stay ahead of competition and make necessary profit to sustain an organisation is for them to innovate.

However, in a rapidly changing marketing environment, organisations may find themselves having to overcome barriers.

Potential barriers to innovation

These can include:

- **Lack of commitment** from senior management.
- **Failure to gather information** or to effectively communicate it.
- **Lack of understanding of customer needs** and competitor activities in the market.
- **Internal issues and blockages** eg politics or an ineffective organisational structure that hinders communication.
- **Lack of resources** ie insufficient investment.
- **Slow new product development** ie new products beaten to the market by competitors.

Therefore, an organisation needs to carry out an innovation audit to understand where they stand before being able to improve there upon.

Improving innovation

Drummond and Ensor suggest an innovation audit should assess the following four key aspects of the organisation.

1 **The current organisational climate** – This can be split into two areas.

   (a) Attitude surveys of key areas that affect creativity.

   (b) Use of the technique of metaphorical description. Individuals are asked to describe their organisation in terms of a metaphor eg 'This organisation is not a motor boat but a super tanker. It takes a long time for it to change direction'.

2 **Current performance in delivering innovation** – These hard measures can be measured through some of the following.

   - Employee turnover
   - Customer satisfaction ratings
   - Innovation value matrix
   - The rate of new product development in the last three years. (This should highlight the total innovation developments over that period and the success rate should be analysed.)

3 **Reviewing policies and practices that support innovation** – For example, rewards for innovative ideas. Good examples in practice are: Unilever Best Foods, encourage employees to spend three days inside consumer homes to learn more about them and 3M allows employees to spend 15% of their time working on projects of their choice.

4 **Balance of cognitive styles of the senior management team** – The idea is to have a mix of cognitive styles in the senior management team that will influence the businesses' orientation towards creativity and innovation.

The next step is for the organisation to create a culture that embraces change and innovation.

Enabling innovation

This should be designed essentially to overcome the obstacles discussed above. *Drummond and Ensor's* model below describes the conditions required for innovation to take place.

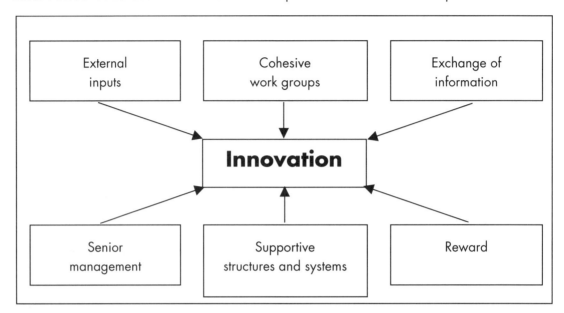

- **Teamwork** – A vital ingredient in the success of innovation. It is essential to have a combination of skills and functions eg marketing, research and design. Innovation flourishes where good working relationships exist and frequent communication is maintained.

- **Exchange of information** – An exchange of information and ideas must be encouraged. An open flow of communication can contribute greatly to creativity and enhance teamwork.

- **External inputs** – This refers to being focused on market trends, customer perception, technological development and competitor activities. All are vital as inputs into the process.

- **Senior management** – They have a significant role to play by being committed to long-term growth as opposed to short-term profit. This gives nourishment to innovation and creativity. Another way is to create the right organisational climate for senior management to 'live the vision'.

- **Support and systems** – Effective communication networks eg intranet; computer aided design; project management structures etc help to support innovation.

- **Reward** – Recognition for innovation helps generate ideas and foster a collaborative atmosphere.

Key to success

A key to organisational success is to increase the rate of which new products and modifications are brought into the market. Some examples to increase the rate are shown below.

- **Multi-functional teams** to plan and develop new products can be formed.

- **Parallel activities** in the new product development process can be used.

- **'Gates'** can be **built into the development process**, encouraging evaluation and resources allocated for the next stage at each step.

- **Customers can be involved** in generating ideas, evaluation and testing phases of new product development.

- A **clear strategic direction** for the organisation's new product development activities should be set.
- **Learning should be managed** and ensure all relevant information is freely available to members of the development team.

In other words, time is of the essence, effectiveness of processes, the right cultural climate and support systems is vital in improving an organisation's ability to innovate.

29 Planning for growth

> *Tutorial note*. The key topic here is human resource planning this has been a frequent topic of exam questions in recent years. Although this looks like an unstructured question, note that you are asked to (a) identify the HRP issues, (b) outline how you intend to *identify* the company's needs for marketing skills *and* (c) outline how you intend to *meet* those needs.

REPORT: GROWTH OBJECTIVES AND HUMAN RESOURCE PLANNING ISSUES OF PLANNED EXPANSION

To: The Managing Director
By: Your Name, HR Manager
Date: [as appropriate]

1 Introduction

As discussed at the last management meeting, our human resource plan needs to be updated to take account of the revised corporate objective of 35% growth in the next two years. This report addresses the human resource requirements for marketing: developing and promoting an extended product range and maintaining quality service to an expanded customer base.

2 Human resource planning issues

Expansion creates the demand for more human resources (people's time, knowledge and skills) which may need to be met through external recruitment and/or the training, development and redeployment of existing staff. There are certain key HRP issues for our business.

    2.1 The **lead time required** to recruit and train staff in the highly technical software market means that we cannot afford to take an *ad hoc* or reactive approach to filling skill requirements as they arise: there is a need for immediate proactive planning if we are to have the right people in the right place at the right time as our expansion progresses.

    2.2 At the same time, our market and technological environment are subject to **swift** (and sometimes unforeseeable) **change and innovation**. It is important to develop a human resource plan that is flexible, and to review and update it regularly as our corporate strategies change.

    2.3 A range of marketing skills may be required to reach our expansion objective.

        ■ Development of an expanded product range, to sustain growing demand consistent with our marketing orientation, requires effective market research, feedback gathering and database interrogation skills to ascertain the market's emerging needs and wants.

- Expansion of the product range requires the support of marketing communication skills in managing the promotion mix and network relationships (particularly with distributors and retail outlets) in order to maximise both push and pull opportunities to reach customers.
- Expansion of the product range requires updated product and technical knowledge for customer service and after-sales support.
- Expansion of the customer base requires additional resources in customer relations – and perhaps also new skills to develop and manage the customer base in different ways: the more thorough use of database and relationship marketing, for example, to leverage sales of the new products to existing customers.

2.4 The planned expansion represents fast and potentially radical change: human resource planning will need to be carried out with an awareness of change management issues – including informing, consulting, training and resourcing existing employees to accept and buy into changes.

3 Identifying appropriate marketing skills

As noted in Section 2.3 above, a range of marketing skills are required for successful expansion – but we cannot afford to guess at what the specific skill gaps might be. I propose a systematic approach to HRP, using the following methods.

3.1 Analysis of **skills likely to be required** for the expansion
- Objective setting and key task/role definition for each marketing activity, in relation to the sub-unit objectives prepared during corporate planning.
- Benchmarking: researching the experience of other expanding organisations in our market

3.2 Audit of skills currently available within the organisation
- Analysis of job descriptions, person specifications and competency profiles
- Analysis of staff performance appraisals and post-training assessments

3.3 Analysis of skills available in the employment market
- Assess the take-up (and relevance to our objectives) of educational opportunities in target recruitment areas
- Assess the availability of skilled labour in the market (eg via industry reports and recruitment analysts in target areas)
- Assess market and competitor activity which will affect the competition for skills

3.4 Identify the gap between forecast demand [(a) above] and current supply of skills [(b) above].

3.5 Evaluate alternative means of closing this gap, given the benefits and costs of obtaining skills from the *internal* and *external* employment markets.

4 Means of ensuring the required skill supply

Once we have identified specific skill gaps, we can systematically investigate opportunities for acquiring and retaining the skills we need. There are a number of broad approaches that may be taken.

4.1 **Training, development and/or redeployment of staff** to meet anticipated requirements. This has the advantage of synergy, building on the product knowledge, cultural acceptance and loyalty of existing staff. Development opportunities, positively communicated managed, may also be powerful motivators. If we can adopt a multi-skilling approach to development and task structuring, we may be able to create adaptive, flexible teams which can be redeployed to meet foreseen *and* unforeseen demands as the expansion proceeds.

4.2 **Improved staff retention programmes** in order to avoid turnover of staff with required skills: this may involve attention to a number of people management issues, including motivation and reward, and leadership style. Exit interviews should immediately be implemented to identify why skilled staff leave.

4.3 **External recruitment** to meet anticipated requirements which cannot be cost-effectively met within the organisation. This has the advantage of adding 'new blood' to the business at a time when we are looking to change and innovate. However, it also dilutes the loyalty base of the workforce and may exacerbate change-related insecurity. Costs and benefits will need to be weighed up for different skill areas and levels.

4.4 **Outsourcing**. New marketing activities (for example, if we adopt more thorough Customer Relationship Management) can be outsourced to specialist agencies. Some existing activities, such as market research, may also be outsourced, allowing use to retain and redeploy existing staff where appropriate.

4.5 **Automation**. It should be remembered that one option is to increase productivity *without* necessarily increasing human resources: some market research and CRM tasks, for example, can be computerised, using database, automated call handling and so on.

5 Conclusion

Resource Planning needs to be a systematic exercise, fully integrated with the corporate objectives of the business as a whole. I look forward to discussing the above ideas with you and the various department managers at our next meeting.

30 Managing outside suppliers

Article (Marketing Business): 'Getting to grips with outsourcing'

From: A Marketing Director

1 **Introduction**

In this world of increasing globalisation and faster change, organisations need to continually **review their core competences** and to consider which marketing activities might be better **outsourced**.

Generally speaking, if an outside supplier can do a better job than your own company at an equivalent cost, or an equivalent job at a lower cost, then a switch should be made.

When reviewing the possibilities, the process should cover:

- The types of outside marketing resources the company could use
- How contenders for these services should be briefed
- How the selected suppliers should be managed and controlled

2 **Types of outside marketing resources we could use**

2.1 **Consultants**

There are a great many management and marketing consultants in the UK. The CIM, for example, provides a comprehensive service. Some consultants specialise in design, research or promotion.

2.2 **Marketing research agencies**

Not many organisations have all the in-house facilities needed to cater for their total information requirements. Nearly all organisations find it necessary to outsource surveys to specialists.

2.3 **Promotional agencies**

There are a great variety of promotional agencies, ranging from advertising agencies to agencies specialising in sales promotion, PR and telesales/telemarketing. With sales promotion there is a range of specialists in packaging design, POS display material, exhibition services, mail order and so on. The opportunities provided by the Internet have given rise to a number of agencies specialising in website design.

2.4 **Marketing training organisations**

Universities and professional bodies can be used to improve the skills of marketing departments and provide specialist courses.

2.5 **Full-service agencies**

These endeavour to supply the full range of marketing services from consultancy to marketing research and promotion and are particularly suitable for smaller organisations.

2.6 **New product development**

This is a controversial issue and covers a very wide field, but pharmaceutical companies, for example, will often subcontract at least part of their extremely costly and risky laboratory research to a number of selected specialists, such as biotechnology companies.

3 **How outside suppliers should be briefed**

3.1 The **briefing** of outside suppliers is of paramount importance, since an inadequate brief will lead to misunderstandings.

3.2 We need to adopt a position of mutual **trust** with our suppliers. Being able to trust them should be the most important criterion for doing business. We can then provide them with a full statement of our requirements.

3.3 Our detailed requirements should include a full **specification** of the services we are seeking, the standards we expect and any special conditions of contract such as penalty clauses.

3.4 We should make suppliers aware that competitive tenders will be sought.

3.5 Suppliers should be given the right to query the detail of our requirements, and to make suggestions for any amendments.

3.6 An indication of the **budget** and any other limitations should be provided where appropriate.

3.7 Suppliers should be made fully aware of the **timescales**.

3.8 Finally, all suppliers should be made aware that their performance will be **appraised**.

4 How suppliers might be controlled and measured

A decision has to be made whether to **apply controls selectively**. A supplier we use irregularly or for small amounts should not be subjected to the same degree of control as a supplier whose goods/services are a major item of expenditure.

However, the answer cannot depend on spend alone. We could, for example, be spending relatively little on an agency on concept testing for a proposed new product. However, this proposed new product could be vital to our future and therefore the agency could require stricter control than a supplier of high cost materials who has proved to be highly dependable for a number of years.

The nature of the control should perhaps be different according to the nature of the product/service being bought. For some materials suppliers we would, for example, have scientific tests on quality and maintain records of deliveries late/on time/before time. However, for our advertising agency, control might be more informal and based on frequent personal meetings.

Bearing in mind the above difficulties in setting standards and the rating of performance, I would recommend the following controls.

- Supplier's name
- Type of goods/services supplied
- Estimated annual expenditure
- Record of complaints made by us
- Record of actions taken by supplier

Performance standard
Rating (scale 0 to 10)
Notes

- Quality of product/service
- Reliability
- Prices relative to competitors
- Working relationships
- Overall
- Special terms and conditions relative to this supplier
- Recommended special controls, if any
- Recommended frequency of review
- Person responsible for review, position/department

There should, following the initial review, be a **rolling system of reviewing** outside suppliers, on the recommended frequencies and against the agreed standards. **Formal ratings are preferred to informal measures**. The frequency of the reviews and the nature of the standards set should be changed in accordance with circumstances.

All suppliers should be informed about our review system and invited to comment/co-operate.

5 Conclusion

There are of course a number of implications for other business functions in the decision to extend the number of subcontracted marketing activities. Not least of these are the implications for staffing and finance. It will be necessary for me to meet with co-directors before taking any further action on this organisational issue.

Answer Bank

31 Relationship marketing

Perhaps the most talked about concept in the field of marketing is relationship marketing. Relationship marketing can be defined as the overt attempt of exchange partners to build a long-term association in which purposeful co-operation occurs, mutual dependence occurs and social, as well as structural bonds, are developed.

In many respects, the relationships that result resemble marriages. As in marriages, organisational relationships move through a series of **stages**.

(a) Awareness of each other — First meeting
(b) Exploration — First date
(c) Expansion — Going 'steady'
(d) Commitment — Marriage
(e) Dissolution — Divorce

As in marriages, managers in the organisational buying centre must recognise that give and take will exist with suppliers. Similarly, the salesforce must be willing to adjust rapidly to the changing needs of its customers. Managers must recognise that, as in marriages, the dissolution phase will be much more difficult than in traditional contractual exchanges.

Another critical element in building long-term relationships is trust. Relationship trust can be defined as a willingness to rely on an exchange partner in whom one has confidence. Thus, to reveal trust in a relationship, the members must reveal vulnerability to each other. In such cases, control of important resources is left with the other member of the exchange. As a result, the exchange members must rely on each other to fulfil their obligations in the exchange. When high levels of trust exist, the exchange process becomes more flexible and less bureaucratic, and legal entanglements are minimised.

32 Quality management

Introduction

To ensure continued success for the organisation, the issue of quality must be addressed. **Quality management** ensures that products or services meet their planned level of quality and conform to specifications. The cost of quality failure can be significant. For example, the cost of destruction caused by radiation contamination of the environment throughout Europe after the explosion at Chernobyl in Russia. is an extreme. However, on a day-to-day basis, in our industry an electrical fault in one of our products could start a **'word-of-mouth'** fallout and thus damage our reputation. Outlined below are three alternative approaches of measurement against a performance standard.

Benchmarking

Benchmarking is the process of improved quality through comparison with another organisation or a different part of the same organisation. Quality improvement can be achieved through **learning from the practices and methods of others** and adopting them for use in the organisation. However, there can be limitations in the transfer of such practices especially where different cultures are involved (*Needle*).

Benchmarking falls into three general areas.

- **Competitive analysis** – This may involve reviewing competitor's strategies, operations and activities so that the organisation can improve its performance.

- **Best Practice** – Is determining the best way of undertaking an activity. This could involve examining activities in unrelated areas of business or industry eg our electronics business against a mail order company in order to improve our stock control. Also, we could look within our own organisation and identify best practice and utilise it throughout the organisation.

- **Performance standards** – Targets to be met or surpassed eg if the average conversion rate in our part of the industry sector for enquiries converted into sales was say 1:50, and ours was say 1:70, this would indicate that we have a performance problem.

The process of benchmarking

To undertake the process of benchmarking, the 'Deming Cycle' can be applied. This four-stage approach is illustrated below.

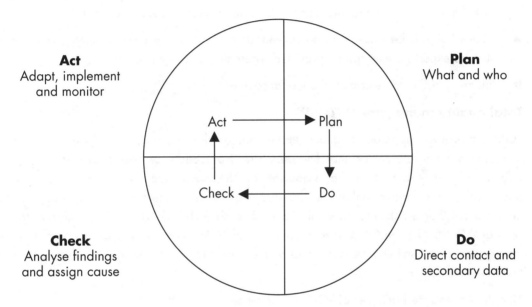

The Deming cycle applied to benchmarking *(Source: Drummond and Ensor)*

- **Plan** – Identify what to study and who or what should act as the benchmark eg benchmark against competitors, other acknowledged leaders or successful internal standards.

- **Do** – Conduct research by accessing secondary data to establish standards and actions or, have direct contact with the possible benchmarking organisation.

- **Check** – Analyse the data and establish the extent of performance gaps identifying the assignable causes for such gaps.

- **Act** – Lessons learned are adapted and applied in order to improve performance.

Business process re-engineering (BPR)

This is a radical approach to quality improvement with the aim of **integrating all activities** of the organisation to focus on the customer. It involves the re-think of all aspects of operations in terms of **cost, quality, speed** and **service standards**. The results often include a **deliberate restructuring** of the organisation that involves nothing short of dramatic improvements (*Needle*). For example, when Transco was first formed out of British Gas, the first re-engineering process was to de-layer the structure from 17 to 7 levels of management from the 'shop floor' to the 'top'. In other words, re-engineering involves the question: 'If we were a new company, how would we run the operation?'

Principles of BPR

- Processes should be designed to achieve a desired outcome rather than focusing on existing tasks.

- Personnel who use the output from a process should perform the process eg personnel ordering their own resources thereby eliminating the need for a separate purchasing function.

- Information processing should be included in the work that produces the information.

- Geographically dispersed resources should be treated as if they are centralised eg economies of scale through central negotiation of supply contracts, without losing the benefits of decentralisation, such as flexibility and responsiveness.

- Parallel activities should be linked rather than integrated. This would involve eg co-ordination between teams working on different aspects of a single process.

- 'Doers' should be allowed to be self-managing (in essence empowerment). Decision aids such as expert systems can be provided where they are required.

- Information should be captured once, at source.

Total quality management (TQM)

TQM is a strategic approach to quality that embraces all members of the organisation and aims to create a corporate culture that **focuses on the needs of the customer** by building quality into every aspect of the organisation. The advantages are a cost saving for the organisation and added value for the customer. It is a method of long-term continuous improvement that is linked to national standards such as BS 5750 and international standards such as ISO 9000 (*Needle*). Common criticisms of TQM however, include: its association with introduction of a cumbersome bureaucracy and the problems of introducing such a systems in low trust cultures.

Needle suggests the principles of TQM are as follows:

- It is a **top – down management philosophy** that focuses on the needs of the customer.

- **Key values tend to include customer awareness**; getting it right first time; continuous improvement and team working.

- It **comprises a quality plan**, that offers a structured, disciplined approach to quality and incorporates a number of systems, tools and techniques. Particular emphasis is given to the collection and analysis of information and to employee training.

- It **covers all parts of the organisation** and often involves those organisations in the supply chain. Relationships between departments in the same organisation, as well as those between firms in the supply chain, are governed by detailed service level agreements.

- TQM is **culturally based**. Involvement of all employees is central to its philosophy. Its statements abound with references to teamwork and creative thinking and often contain slogans about empowerment of adding value.

- TQM **focuses on the elimination of costs associated with control and failure**. These are seen as signs of poor quality. Instead the emphasis is on the prevention through the involvement of all employees. In this way all costs are reduced.

- Through its focus on **continuous improvement**, TQM is essentially a long-term approach.

Conclusion

All of the above concepts have their advantages and disadvantages for an organisation. Should you require further information in this regard, I would be pleased to provide it.

33 Expenditure

'Money Well Spent'

by

Patricia Verna

All good marketing management teams will be able to respond to a barrage of questions like: Are the communications working? Are they effective? Are we getting good value? Could we get it more cost effectively? The amount of money any company spends on **marketing communications** and advertising in particular, is absolutely crucial.

The intention of this article therefore, is to provide a guide to proportioning investment in marketing communications. In so doing, it is important to define what marketing communication is and what it purports to do. Thereafter an understanding is developed of the different approaches to budgeting.

Marketing communications is the success of any organisation but can cost a great deal. Communications to various audiences 24 hours of every day via the Internet, TV, radio, printed media, billboards, buses and bus shelters etc are made to the following:

- Customers
- Dealers
- Employees
- Shareholders
- Financial advisers
- Suppliers
- Local communities
- Competitors
- Media
- Many other interested parties

The level of interaction will vary in intensity with each of these audiences depending upon a number of variables. However, marketing communications is about creating and sustaining a dialogue with each of these stakeholder audiences as highlighted in the drip model below.

Differentiates between competing offerings helping consumers to decide which exchanges to make.

Reminds customers of the benefits of past transactions and so convince them that they should enter into a similar exchange.

Informs and makes potential customers aware of an organisation's offering.

Persuades current and potential customers of the desirability of entering into an exchange relationship.

Examples to illustrate this involve British Airways who invested over £60m in their corporate re-branding exercise in order to be identified as a global, not British, airline. Kellogg's, Nestlé, Cadbury's, Unilever and the many other 'fast moving consumer goods' (fmcg) manufacturers invest millions each year on advertising in order to maintain and/or grow their market share.

Organisations in the business-to-business sector spend much less on advertising but more on personal selling and sales support.

It has been learnt over the years that choosing the right level of investment is important but it is not a science. In view of this, methods in deciding budgets have been developed, some of which include:

- **Percentage of sales**
- **Matching the competition**
- **Objective and task**
- **All you can afford**

All of these methods have flaws but recent research has indicated a growing trend towards objective and task as this much more closely matches up with at least having sufficient funds to meet the marketing objectives.

Another technique involves the **advertising/sales (A/S) ratio** that is calculated by working out the total amount spent on advertising for each market sector as a proportion of the sales in that market. This provides an industry benchmark in order that it can be understood whether investment is above or below the industry average. However, there are severe limitations to this approach. This ratio although it is useful, does not provide the complete answer as it focuses only on advertising. There is also a need to use sales promotion, direct and interactive marketing, public relations, the sales force plus internal marketing communication activities.

It was reported that Procter & Gamble wanted to reduce their amount of advertising spend from 25% to 20% and use the 'savings' to fund price-offs in order to compete more effectively with their own-label competitors. A counter view from the company was that they wanted to use their advertising and media expenditure much more efficiently yet maintain their overall visibility. This was **a strong strategic approach** and it courted much criticism and debate.

Thus by gauging the percentage of an organisation's communication spend against the total spent by all others in the market, one is able to determine what is known as **share of voice**. These figures can be compared to the organisation's market share and through analysis it can be determined how much should be spent to achieve the desired market share. Whilst this is intuitively appealing there are some real difficulties in making this work.

In contrast, **PIMS (Profit Impact of Marketing Strategy)** is a database system that uses actual data from real organisations across a variety of industries and market sectors. Through analysis of the database it is possible to determine what return on investment can be achieved based upon a number of variables. Depending upon whether a company is market leader, number two or just another player, it is possible to make judgements about issues such as the level of above and below-the-line promotional expenditure, or the right amount of trade communications.

A number of methods can be used to compare the outcomes. It should be determined what **objectives** need to be achieved and the **strategies** to be used to achieve the stated objectives. The available strategic options are: **push** (trade) and **pull** (consumer) and **profile** (corporate) communication strategies. The most effective approach is a combination of the three rather than in isolation. At this stage necessary changes are likely to be identified and made along with determining the costs before putting it all into action.

Pedigree Pet foods, for example, have said that after the tins and the cost of the meat, the third most important factor to be measured and evaluated was the cost of the media and level of discounts used to advertise their pet food products. This further serves to demonstrate that the level of communication spend can be a very significant part of an organisation's activities and thus needs a strategic perspective.

In order to grow and thrive it will be even more important for an organisation not only to make good use of **marketing communications**, but to also invest in communications in order that it maintains dialogue with the right audience, using the right message, at the right price and at the right time.

34 Feedback and control system

Control in a planning system has two aspects. It **monitors and corrects current performance**. Feedback received is fed back into the next planning cycle. The factors that should be taken into account in the development of a marketing feedback and control system are illustrated in a simple model shown below.

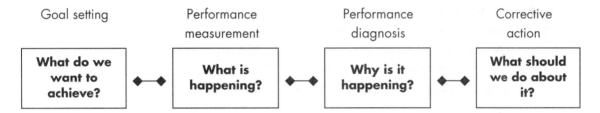

Goal setting is the role of the planning element of strategic marketing. Ideally, the standards set will have been developed within an understanding of what the organisation is able to deliver. Specifically, the following should be taken into account:

- The type of control information required (financial and non-financial)
- The methods used to collect the information (audits, budgets and variance analysis)
- Who requires the information?
- What form the information should take? (weekly, monthly annual reports, presentations, continuous computer based data)
- The information systems required
- The resource implications
- The behavioural implications of controlling peoples' activities

This final point is less obvious, but very important if the control system is to work effectively. The **involvement of a range of managers and personnel** in the **evaluation** process is vital together with the need for **good communication**, both within the marketing unit and between departments. Marketing feedback and control systems need to recognise the volatile nature of human beings and that problems of unsatisfactory feedback and control can occur. Therefore to ensure effective implementation, the feedback and control system will **require internal marketing** to employees. The purpose of this is to inform and motivate employees and sustain effective co-ordination of marketing activities.

Feedback and control information can be used in five distinct areas of operation.

Below is a table to highlight these areas and the techniques used to control them.

Types of analysis	Used to control
1 **Financial analysis** Ratio analysis Variance analysis Cash budgeting Capital budgeting and capital expenditure audit	Elements of profitability Costs or review Cash flow Investment
2 **Market/sales analysis** Demand analysis Market share or penetration Sales targets Sales budget	Competitive standing Sales effectiveness Efficiency in use of resources for selling
3 **Physical resource analysis** Capacity fill Yield Product inspection	Plant utilisation Materials utilisation Quality
4 **Human Resources analysis** Work measurement Output measurement Labour turnover	Productivity Workforce stability
5 **Analysis of systems** Management by objectives Network analysis	Implementation of strategy Resource, planning and scheduling

The **market/sales and distribution analysis** as illustrated above, is particularly relevant for marketing planning. Information can be gathered through audits/ budgeting or variance analysis.

Marketing audits allow for regular monitoring of the successful implementation of **marketing plans**. For example, a marketing manager might use the information from the mix audit to recognise that communication targets are not being reached. From this point, corrective action would be needed in the form of a campaign review and redevelopment.

Budgeting is the most common form of control. It is financial in nature and very useful when applied to marketing implementation. Budgets tend to be short-term and based on the annual plan for achievement of the year's profit and sales forecasts. Monthly deviations from the sales plan tend to require **tactical alterations** eg in the form of price increases or decreases to influence demand. Where budgeting is longer-term, this is more appropriate for monitoring strategic decisions such as product portfolio management. For example, in the product plan there will be products identified as question marks or potential stars.

Using the BCG Matrix model, the position of each product will suggest how much close monitoring and control is needed. Information on high-risk or high-potential new products would be used to manage the risk, and to ensure sales forecasts are accurate to avoid back order or production problems.

Variance analysis leads on from budgeting and involves detailed analysis of the difference between actual and expected results. This sort of control information might possibly be used to consider sales-price variances, sales-quantity variances, profit variances and market share variances.

Many marketing activities are not evaluated or controlled but are assumed to be effective. Marketers tend to enjoy **planning** and **tactical implementation** but shy away from feedback on the results of their initiatives. This is short sighted as it severely limits learning from experience and can, at worst, result in inefficient and ineffective marketing plans.

35 Balanced scorecard

Introduction

Kaplan and Norton suggest that the **balanced scorecard** is a set of measures that gives top managers a fast but comprehensive view of their business while traditional financial account measures like return on investment and earnings per share can give misleading signals. In today's competitive environment where it is necessary for **continuous improvement and innovation**, a failure to convert improved operational performance into improved financial performance should send executives back to rethink the company's strategy or its implementation plans.

From a marketing point of view, the balanced scorecard approach enables all the vital perspectives (**customer**; internal business; financial; **innovation and learning**) not just the financial ones to be taken into account. In fact, customer and innovation, relate directly to marketing.

Customer perspective

Given that organisation mission statements usually identify customer satisfaction as a key corporate goal, they need to ask themselves: **How do customers see us**? The balanced scorecard can translate this into specific measures. To this end, customer concerns fall into four categories.

1 **Time** – Lead time is the time it takes a business to meet customer needs from receiving an order to delivering a product.

2 **Quality** – Quality measures not only include defect levels – although these should be minimised by TQM – but accuracy in forecasting.

3 **Performance** of the product eg how often does the paper shredder break down?

4 **Service** – How long will it take for a problem to be rectified? (eg If the paper shredder breaks down, how long will it take the maintenance engineer to arrive?)

Internal business perspective

This perspective identifies the business processes that have the greatest impact on customer satisfaction eg quality and employee skills.

- Organisations should attempt to identify and measure their **distinctive competences** and the critical technologies they need to ensure continued leadership ie which processes should they excel at?

- To achieve these goals, **performance measures must relate to employee behaviour**, and tie in the strategic direction with employee action.

- It is necessary to have an information system to enable executives to measure performance. This **executive information system** will enable managers to make contact with lower level information.

Innovation and learning perspective

The following question needs to be asked: '**Can we continue to improve and create value**?' While the customer and internal process perspectives identify the *current* parameters for competitive success, the organisation needs to learn and to innovate to **satisfy future needs**. To this end, the following needs to be addressed:

- How long does it take to develop new products?
- How quickly does the organisation climb the experience curve to make new products?
- What percentage of revenue comes from new products?
- How many suggestions are made by employees and are acted upon?
- What are employee attitudes?
- Can the company identify measures for training and long-term investment?

Financial perspective

Measure	For	Against
Profitability	Easy to calculate and understand	Ignores the size of the investment.
Return on investment (profit/capital)	Accounting measure: easy to calculate and understand. Takes size of investment into account. Widely used	<ul><li>Ignores risk</li><li>Easy to manipulate eg managers may postpone necessary capital investment to improve ration</li><li>What are 'assets'? eg do brands count?</li><li>Only really suited to products in the maturity phase of the life cycle, rather than others that are growing fast</li></ul>
Residual income	Head Office levies an interest charge for the use of asset	Not related to the size of investment except indirectly
Earnings per share	Relates the firm's performance to needs of its shareholder	Shareholders are more concerned about future expectations; ignores capital growth as a measure of shareholders' wealth
DCF measures	Relates performance to investment appraisal used to take the decision; cash flows rather than accounting profits are better predictors of shareholder wealth	<ul><li>Practical difficulties in predicting future cash flows of a whole company</li><li>Difficulty in separating cash flows for products that share resources</li></ul>

Linkages

A failure to view all the measures as a whole may lead to **disappointing results**. For example, increasing productivity can mean that fewer employees are needed for a given level of output ie quality improvements can create excess capacity. However, these improvements have to be exploited eg by increasing sales. The financial element of the balanced scorecard reminds executives that improved quality, response time, productivity or new products, benefit the company only when they are translated into improved financial results, or if they enable the organisation to obtain a sustainable competitive advantage.

36 Budgeting

Introduction

Budgeting is the setting of standards for income and expenditure and establishing mechanisms through which all activities can be measured. This process translates marketing strategy into financial terms and is a way to evaluate and control. Budgeting serves not only to quantify plans but, allocate and co-ordinate resources, highlight areas of critical importance and assign responsibility.

Drummond and Ensor suggest that budgeting has two elements:

- **Resource allocation**
- **Political process (negotiating to obtain the required resources)**

Before managers can prepare a budget, there are fundamental requirements that need to be met. These are:

- **Budget guidelines** - The policy and procedures relating to budget formulation must be understood. These set out assumptions, methods and presentational requirements. Also in terms of marketing resources, it will depend on the degree to which the organisation is marketing orientated as to the amount allocated.

- **Cost Behaviour** - Management must understand what drives costs within their area of responsibility. Additionally, it is important to be clear on how costs are allocated eg what is the basis of overhead cost allocation?

- **Timescale** - A specific time period needs to be set. This could be for a fixed budgetary period, such as a financial year, or could simply be a rolling budget. This is where the budget is split into manageable periods of time, and outlined forecasts are updated at regular intervals. New periods are added as the budget progresses.

- **Objectives**. What are we aiming to achieve and how is it being assessed?

Corporate or departmental goals should be translated into resources and subsequent budgetary requirements. However, if marketing is not considered to have a major impact on corporate success, then it is unlikely to have much say in how much money is allocated to its activity. This suggests that marketing is considered as a function of the organisation rather than a philosophy.

Problems in constructing budgets

Some of the problems encountered in setting a budget are:

- Difficulties in identifying **principle budget factors** - Sales and resources demand may not be known.

- **Unpredictability** in economic conditions of prices of inputs.

- **Inflation** – It might be difficult to estimate future price levels for materials, expenses and salaries.

- **Managers might be reluctant to budget accurately** and overstate their expected expenditure. By having a budget that is larger than necessary they are not likely to overspend thus, avoiding the charge of overspending on budget.

Methods of setting the marketing budget

Most organisations adopt a historic way of setting a budget based on previous financial data where adjustments can be made for factors like inflation and levels of activity. This basic incremental model using the previous year's figures, for example, acts as a base and allows for adding or subtracting an amount based on some business factor. However, managers often have to justify their actions and challenge proposed changes.

A selection of other methods is shown below.

Method	Comment
Competitive parity	Fixing promotional expenditure in relation to the expenditure incurred by competitors. Generally, this is unsatisfactory because it suggests your competitor's decision is a good one.
The task method (or object and task)	The marketing task for the organisation is set and a promotional budget is prepared which will help to ensure that the objective is achieved. A problem occurs if the objective is achieved only by paying out more on promotion than the extra profits obtained would justify.
Communication stage model	These are based on the idea that the link between promotion and sales cannot be measured directly, but can be measured by means of intermediate stages (for example, increase in awareness, comprehension, and then intention to buy).
All you can afford	Crude and unscientific, but commonly used. The organisation simply takes a view on what it thinks it can afford to spend on promotion given that it would like to spend as much as it can.
Investment	The advertising and promotions budget can thus be designed around the amount felt necessary to maintain a certain brand value
Rule-of thumb, non-scientific method	These include the percentage of sales, profits etc.

37 Royal Shakespeare Company

REPORT
IMPROVING MANAGEMENT-ACTOR RELATIONS

The role of internal communications in enhancing the RSC brand
Compiled by Your Name, Marketing Manager,
For the meeting of the Board of Directors on [date]

I   Background

This report was compiled at the request of the Board of Directors to address the key issues of internal communications and their impact on the morale and motivation of actors. Conversations with directors and media interviews have suggested that some actors are uncertain about the RSC's vision and the reasons behind recent changes. This is of

Answer Bank

considerable concern, since actors are a theatre company's finest brand ambassadors. This is a question not just of promoting the RSC brand through its employees, but of establishing a positive **employer** brand.

II Internal Communications Audit

Following the Board's decision to undertake an objective audit of the company's internal communications, I would make the following recommendations.

(a) Since the objectivity of the analysis was agreed to be the key to its effectiveness, I suggest that we employ an HR or communications consultant (such as People in Business) to undertake the study. This would enable us to think outside the scope of our current culture and methods. It would also enable study of our managerial style and skills, and the actors' perceptions of management, with greater freedom and honesty than if the study were undertaken by management itself.

(b) The study should take place over a relatively brief period – say, four to six weeks. This would have the benefit of economy (a significant factor, in light of our state subsidy) and minimal disruption.

(c) The consultants should be asked to undertake the following (subject to their expert advice).

   (i) **Analyse** the overall internal communications **structure**: that is, the mechanisms and channels used for communication between managers and actors. The frequency, suitability and efficiency of various channels and mechanisms (written, oral and face-to-face) should be assessed.

   (ii) **Review** all written communications with actors over the past year. This would include standing communications (such as employment manuals, actor contracts, tour schedules and information sheets), occasional communications (such as bulletins, communiqués and invitation to company events) and individual communications (all correspondence).

   The frequency, subject matter, tone and style of communications should be assessed, with a view to evaluating efficiency, effectiveness and relational/image aspects.

   (iii) Sit in on all meetings relating to the acting companies, in order to **assess** managers' roles, attitudes, interpersonal skills and relational styles; the communication agenda of such meetings; and the relationship between management and actors (where applicable).

   (iv) **Interview** senior and selected middle managers, to assess the managerial values and style being communicated from the top of the organisation.

   (v) Call and conduct a series of **focus-group meetings** with different acting companies and stage managers, involving a cross-section of the actors working at the time. The purpose of these meetings would be to explore the actors' perceptions of management's role and relational style and the efficiency and effectiveness of formal communication mechanisms.

   (vi) **Interview** a selection of actors who have previously worked with the RSC but are not currently under contract. Since we want the best actors to take repeat contracts with us, after intervals of work for our competitors, it is essential to assess how we communicate with them on an on-going, relationship-building basis.

III Induction programme for new actors

The induction issues are twofold.

1 Actors' perceptions of the company's goals – and the role and values of its management – are confused, following the period of change.

2 Actors' expectations do not accurately reflect the demands of the RSC's rigorous rehearsal schedule and touring life.

It is essential that actors' expectations and perceptions are managed before problems arise. Given short contracts and tour schedules, a quick and flexible approach to induction is recommended as follows.

(a) A welcome pack should be prepared for despatch to actors as soon as they have been contracted. This would set out:

   (i) The vision and goals of the RSC, beyond those of making a success of each production: for example, national accessibility and added value for stakeholders

   (ii) The rewards of working for the RSC. While honesty about limited financial rewards is required, the pack should also emphasise intrinsic rewards such as excellence, collaboration with stimulating directors, training opportunities for people to enhance their vocal and movement skills and so on

   (iii) Explanation of the role of management in the company, emphasising managerial support for theatrical excellence and accessibility

   (iv) Details of the rehearsal policy and schedule of the acting companies: hours, rotating repertoire, number of performances per week, understudying responsibilities and so on

   (v) Explanation of touring schedules and demands. It should be possible to describe touring conditions realistically without damaging morale: perhaps through humorous anecdotes by some of our more famous actors

(b) This should be followed up with face-to-face meetings at key induction points.

   (i) On the first day of the actor's contracted period, the manager responsible should give the actor a tour of the theatre, rehearsal facilities, administrative offices and so on; the actor should have an opportunity to put any questions about the information contained in the welcome pack; contractual details should be confirmed and relevant paperwork completed with the manager's help.

   (ii) On the first day of rehearsals for a particular production, the actors should be introduced to the director and to each other by a member of management; managerial support for the production should be explained and emphasised.

   (iii) Opportunities for training and development should be planned early in the contract period, and implemented where possible to fit into the rehearsal and performance schedule.

   (iv) A mentoring scheme may be established, whereby more experienced RSC actors are asked to guide and 'socialise' newcomers to the company.

IV An internal communications plan

Attention will need to be given to the specific areas of communication highlighted by the audit recommended in Section II. However, the following suggestions may be considered.

Consultation and policy development

(a) Management should collaborate with the consultants and staff representatives (including actors' and technicians' unions) to develop a communication policy. This should emphasise the commitment of management and staff to effective relationship and communication; the rights of full-time and freelance staff to information; and the channels and methods available for internal communication and how they should be used.

Structures

(b) Informal communication between actors, and between actors and management, should be facilitated to counterbalance the isolation of touring and the perceived barriers between management, performers and technical personnel. In addition to special social events, we might in the longer term consider the development of a staff canteen and bar to enable all employees to meet and socialise together.

(c) An actors' committee should be formed, to enable the actors to share and convey their views directly to managers.

(d) Employee involvement schemes (such as suggestion schemes) should be developed.

(e) In the longer-term, one of the RSC's associate actors should be invited to join the Board of Directors, so that the actors feel they have genuine representation and investment in the company's decision making.

(f) Meetings should be held on a regular (not necessarily frequent) basis between central management and management of the acting companies and regional theatres, to ensure common goals and employer branding, and to emphasise corporate unity and coherence.

(g) Briefing meetings should be held to inform full-time staff (technicians, craftspeople, coaches and administrators) and where possible freelancers (actors, directors and designers) about the future plans and managerial activity of the company, in areas such as marketing and sponsorship. This may help to break down the perception that increasing managerial activity of this kind is a 'drain on artistic resources' – rather than an essential support to on-stage effort.

Media

(h) The welcome pack suggested in Section III above for the induction of new recruits should also be sent to actors returning to contract, who may not be familiar with the new goals and opportunities.

(i) A newsletter about the company's future plans should be sent to every artist who has worked with the company for the past five years, in order to maintain a sense of involvement and relationship with the company, and to keep the special opportunities offered by the RSC in actors' minds.

(j) Opportunities for training and development (such as voice and movement coaching), complimentary tickets to previews and openings and other in-house benefits should be published in newsletters and posted on staff noticeboards.

Skills development

(k) Where necessary, training in interpersonal skills should be offered to managers, especially those who deal directly with freelance staff such as actors. Interpersonal skills should be included in criteria for managerial recruitment and selection, appraisal, promotion and reward.

Evaluation

(l) The various briefing/feedback/consultation meetings suggested above will allow us to appraise the effectiveness of these improvements. Budgetary constraints permitting, the consultants may also be retained to undertake periodic follow-up monitoring and review of communication and staff attitudes.

The above measures are recommended to improve not only the process of communication, but also the motivation and team spirit of employees – and in particular the freelance actors who are the cornerstone of the RSC on-stage brand.

Positive morale and *esprit de corps* among the actors contributes towards improving the RSC brand in a number of ways.

1. Management theory and anecdote suggests that if management genuinely sets out to understand and respond to the needs of employees, their greater contentment will lead to higher levels of performance. Our experience suggests that this may be particularly true in the artistic field. Enhanced on-stage performance confirms the RSC reputation for high artistic quality.

2. An enhanced organisational reputation allows us to retain current on-staff talent, and to attract returning and future directorial, creative and acting talent. This is particularly important for an organisation like ours that recruits large numbers of people for fixed periods, in the face of increasing competition for a limited pool of quality labour. Our artists are essentially freelancers, which means that: (a) we need to compete for their time and talents; and (b) between contracts with us, they work on other projects where they gain experience of other companies in comparison to our own *and* where they will inevitably influence their fellow artists positively or negatively in regard to their experience with us.

Successful product branding therefore requires successful employer branding, and it is recommended that we give this matter our urgent attention.

38 International Sonatas Hotels

(a) Selecting and building teams

Introduction

The overall aim of the **selection process** is to locate employees who can add value to the organisation. As well as considering the qualities of individuals for the team, consideration should also be given to the international hotel **context** ie their relevant marketing experience and expertise, the **time scale** for developing a team and the **budget** available for training etc. As the new marketing team will be the group's first development in this country and the City Sonata is intended to be a flagship venture, every effort must be made to get it right first time. As good practice and a cost saving measure, this process could be extrapolated to other future City Sonata ventures. When selecting and building the marketing team, the following information will be relevant.

Selecting teams

Faced with developing a team from scratch a **definition of requirements** should be drawn up, a **job analysis** carried out and a **systematic approach** adopted with the aim to 'get the right person' and 'get the person right'. Therefore, a planned recruitment process is needed that will provide the organisation with the best talent, consistent with the needs of the business and its capacity to make full use of the person that it has recruited.

For the purpose of the new team, the Job Description will identify the roles to be filled eg marketing communications, managing promotional campaign, developing a customer care orientation and local media management. It will also include: the job title; location of the job; relationship of the job to other positions both within and outside the marketing team and the main duties and responsibilities of the job.

The decision needs to be made whether to recruit 'in-house' or whether to look for 'new blood'. If recruiting through advertising in the media, for example, adverts should be placed for at least three editions in order to maximise the response and minimise the risk of selecting the wrong candidate. Recruitment can also be carried out through selected agencies. Each responding candidate must be provided with an application pack that includes :-

- A job description
- A person specification
- An Application Form
- An Equal Opportunities Policy
- A Company Information Sheet

The description of the **organisation** shows the strategy and culture of our organisation. This is also a means of communication in attracting the 'right' person to the job. The **job location**, **pay**, **essential requirements** and how to apply should also be specified. The advertisement must be **non-discriminating** on grounds of sex, race or disabilities.

A short list of applications can be drawn up and the selection **interviewing process** can begin. Matching the person to the person specification can be done through **assessment** of a presentation or simulation test, for example, and **based on the Company Interview** Appraisal System. This will include assessment of stipulated criteria that will include:

- Personal Qualities and Relevant Skills
- Acquired Knowledge or Qualifications
- Innate Abilities (how candidates present themselves during the interview)
- Motivation
- Adjustment (ability to demonstrate for example, persuasion, realism, mental perception, self confidence, self control, flexibility, resilience and so on.)

An offer of **placement** can be made to the best candidate during a meeting wherein the **salary**, **additional benefits**, **working hours**, **terms and conditions** (including a six month probationary period to protect both parties) and **starting date** will be agreed. Induction can be carried out on the first day.

Training

Selection of appropriate team members is an ongoing process and they likely to need further development of skills to fulfil their roles. **Training needs** should be identified and a programme set out to meet the team's objectives. As City Sonata are looking for a new marketing team to promote their total service concept which will include conference facilities, the highest standards of comfort, leisure activities etc, the training programme is likely to be based on immediate marketing demands.

Given the time constraints and the fact that it is a new hotel, a large part of training is likely to take place '**on the job**' where more experienced staff may coach the more junior team members.

As the organisation has a **culture** that respects individuality, encourages communication and teamwork and rewards achievement, training should be linked with **career progression**. Training can be offered once performance has been satisfactorily established and the necessary probationary period completed. The organisation may also encourage Chartered Institute of Marketing (CIM) studentship with the view of extending their knowledge and practical skills.

Building

As there is only six months to launch, the team should work together as much as possible and needs to be built by adopting **purposeful and co-ordinated activities**. Ice breaking activities eg social events or away days should be organised to enable members to meet each other, during which they should be encouraged to **share information** about promotional ideas for the new hotel launch in a relaxed and friendly atmosphere. This will provide an environment to **break down barriers** and **build team spirit**.

Teambuilding activities should be held on a regular basis to maintain good practice and allow individuals to develop. This is important as teams go through a **process of development** eg *Tuckman's* forming, storming, norming, performing and adjourning. Therefore, to meet team objectives, teambuilding activities should be seen as a continuous process.

As a **reward** for all the hard work prior to launch, an **incentive** should be offered whereby the team celebrate their successes eg in a specified location.

Motivating the team

Motivating a marketing team is no different to motivating anybody else and all members will bring with them **different morals, values, attitudes and beliefs**. Due to the creative nature of marketing individuals, **allowances** may also need to be made for more extravert and volatile **personality types**. However there are general **guidelines** for motivating a team. Some of these are:

- Offer equal opportunities and treat staff fairly ie non-discrimination.
- Encourage participation in decision-making. This will improve an individual's motivation through self-realisation and empowerment.
- Pay according to clear salary scales and appraisal of performance.
- Establish non-financial incentive schemes such as 'employee of the month'.
- Manage in a participative style without abdicating the responsibility to lead.
- Offer recognition and praise where appropriate.
- Encourage autonomy ie delegate and trust as far as possible.
- New members to the team should be supported and supervised in a non-intrusive manner.
- Set clear objectives and deadlines for reporting back.

With the assistance of the local Human Resource Manager, the team leader has the responsibility to communicate to the team the disproportionate amount of effort and work needed to launch any new venture. The team **need to be reassured** that this adrenalin induced period will settle down however due to the nature of marketing, deadlines will always need to be met.

(b) (i) Internal marketing activities

Introduction

The basis of internal marketing is focusing on the relationship that exists between the organisation and its employees. In its most common usage, internal marketing means the **promotion of a marketing orientation throughout the organisation** and, in particular, creating customer awareness among staff who are not primarily concerned with selling. Even though housekeeping staff at City Sonata Hotels are rarely seen by the guests their work makes a major contribution to the guests' perception of the hotel's quality of service. Therefore, it is important to promote **customer service** to all staff. Thus **the people element of the service marketing mix** is vital in a hotel as all staff need to be convinced of the importance of very high quality customer service.

Development of internal marketing activities

Front line sales and marketing capability at the hotel will probably have to be enhanced. Front line staff (reception, bar staff, restaurant waiting staff, porters) will take greater responsibility for delivering customer satisfaction, and should be given the necessary authority to do so. This will result in greater job satisfaction for them. An 'employee of the month' competition could provide an incentive, with the winning staff member's photograph on display in a prominent place in the hotel's public areas. Proper feedback from guest comments would be essential.

Training will become a major feature of the programme. As well as new recruits, existing staff must be educated in the new methods and approach. The marketing manager will have an input here: internal marketing depends heavily on **commitment at the highest level of management** and it will be part of the marketing manager's job to promote that commitment.

The successful management of staff depends to a great extent upon successful **communication**. Internal marketing has therefore also come to mean the communication aspect of any programme of **change** and, even more simply, **the presentation by management to staff of any kind of information**.

Internal marketing activities for the promotion of a customer care orientation at City Sonata can be thought of in terms of the standard marketing mix.

(1) **Product** under the internal marketing concept is the changing nature of the job to become more customer focused.

(2) **Price** is the balance of psychological costs and benefits involved in adopting the new orientation, plus those elements which have to be given up in order to carry out the new tasks.

(3) Many of the methods used for communication in external marketing may be employed to motivate the hotel employees and influence attitudes and behaviour. Techniques such as multi-media presentations and in-house publications could be used, along with incentive schemes ('employee of the month') to generate changes in employee behaviour.

(4) **Distribution** for internal marketing means e-mails, meetings and conferences, as well as physical means such as noticeboards, which can be used to announce policies and training programmes.

(5) **Physical evidence** refers to tangible items which facilitate delivery or communication of the product. Quality standards such as ISO 9000, for instance, place great emphasis on documentation, such as a staff newsletter.

(6) **Process**, which refers to how a customer actually receives the hotel service, is linked to communication and staff training.

(7) The **people** involved in producing and delivering the product, and those receiving the product, (who will influence the customer's perceptions) are clearly important within the internal marketing process. Communication must be delivered by someone at the right level of authority.

Segmentation and marketing research can also be used in internal marketing. Employees may be grouped according to their service characteristics or tasks in order to organise the promotion of a service orientation.

(ii) **Quality service perception**

Quality can only be defined by customers. A quality service from City Sonata will be achieved when the hotel, through its staff, delivers a service to a specification that satisfies their needs. **Customer expectations** serve as the standard, against which all service experiences are compared. When service performance falls short of customer expectations, dissatisfaction occurs.

The quality of a service is the result of an evaluation process where **consumers compare what they expected to receive with what they perceive that they actually received**. How can City Sonata measure the level of client-perceived service quality?

As a first step, Parasuraman, Zeithaml and Berry developed the most widely applied model of service quality in 1985, highlighting **five gaps** which are the potential hurdles for City Sonata in attempting to deliver high quality service.

Gap 1: Consumer expectations and management perceptions gap

Hotel management may not know what features connote high quality, what features a service must have or what levels of performance are required by customers.

Gap 2: Management perceptions and service quality specification gap

Resource constraints, market conditions and/or management indifference may result in this gap.

Gap 3: Service quality specifications and service delivery gap

Guidelines may exist, but employees may not be willing or able to perform to the specified standards.

Gap 4: Service delivery and external communications gap

Exaggerated promises or lack of information will affect both expectations and perceptions.

Gap 5: Expected service and perceived service gap

This gap was defined as service quality. It is influenced by the preceding four gaps, so if management want to close the gap between performance and expectations it becomes imperative to design procedures for measuring service performance against expectations.

To monitor client perceptions, researchers developed the SERVQUAL questionnaire, which purports to be a global measure of 'Gap 5' across all service organisations. It measures the five **generic criteria that consumers use in evaluating service quality**.

1 **Tangibles**: physical facilities, equipment, appearance of City Sonata personnel

2 **Reliability**: ability to perform the promised service dependably and accurately

3 **Responsiveness**: willingness to help guests and provide prompt service

4 **Assurance**: knowledge and courtesy of hotel employees, and their ability to convey trust and confidence

5 **Empathy**: caring, individualised attention for each guest

City Sonata can ask respondents to give their **expectations** of the service on a graded scale, then to give their evaluation of the **actual service** on the same scale. Service quality can then be calculated as the difference between perception and expectations, weighted for the importance of each item.

Once City Sonata knows how it is performing on each of the dimensions of service quality, it can use a number of methods to try to improve it.

(1) Development of a **customer orientated mission statement** and clear senior management support for quality improvement initiatives

(2) Regular **guest satisfaction research**, including surveys and panels, 'mystery guests', analysis of complaints and benchmarking against other hotels in the Sonatas group

(3) Setting and monitoring **standards** and communicating results

(4) Establishment of systems for guest **complaints and feedback**

(5) Encouragement of **employee participation**, ideas and initiatives, often through the use of quality circles and project teams

(6) **Rewarding** excellent service

39 Family Doctor

(a) **Key internal and external issues facing the practice**

The appointment of an administrator is a response to the unprecedented change that the practice is undergoing. However, it seems that the doctors feel that this is enough and that the problem is mainly administrative.

SWOT analysis brings together an internal appraisal of the organisation's strengths and weaknesses with an analysis of the opportunities and threats seen in the environment. The aim is to neutralise the weaknesses and try and convert threats into opportunities.

Internal issues

Strengths. The practice's strengths include its **reputation** and some of its **clinics**. However, these were developed in the past, and they have to be maintained and nurtured. Furthermore, only two of the partners are concerned about the practice in the **long term**.

Weaknesses. These seem to be in the **internal structure and management** of the practice, not its clinical effectiveness. Although the new administrator sounds very pessimistic, it may be that she has yet to adjust her desire for clear management, as would be expected in the profit-making organisation, with the fact that, in a practice which is a

non-profit making organisation with a variety of objectives, a **dispersal of power amongst various stakeholders** is inevitable, and, in a service which is publicly funded delivering specialist care, even desirable. However, internal deficiencies can be listed as follows.

(i) **Poor information** regarding the practice's performance. This is serious if doctors are to be paid by results.

(ii) **Poor management of support staff** (an area where distinctly managerial skills are desirable).

(iii) The practice has **no mission**, other than the doctor's professional specialisms.

(iv) Staff are resisting change.

Stakeholders

There is a danger that the administrator is trying to impose a managerial model of the organisation on the practice. The administrator has to negotiate with the various stakeholder groups in the practice.

(i) **The partners, as significant stakeholders, are not united.** Only two want to stay around in the long term. The administrator's relationship is complicated by the fact that each partner is her boss. The practice is a minor example of what *Mintzberg* calls a **professional bureaucracy**, in which the operating core is supported, rather than controlled, by the managerial infrastructure.

(ii) The administrator also had problems with the **computer expert** who had **expert** and **resources power** over the practice's computer systems.

(iii) **The practice is a public service.** The regional health authority and the patients (who pay for the service out of their taxation) are stakeholders with legitimate interests.

(iv) There has been **no systematic analysis of customer needs** and requirements in the area (eg does it have a higher than average proportion of elderly people?). This would give some guidance as to their performance targets.

External opportunities and threats

The environment provides opportunities and threats. Unlike a business, the practice is controlled by its customers, the public, through a roundabout route, and the only competitive threat is that of losing patients to competing practices. However, the supplier of resources, the government (as customer as well as a supplier) is able to impose changes in management and technique.

Opportunities include **the liaison with the local Health Authority:** the practice, already an innovator, will have advance information about planned developments and will be able to shape developments. The practice might be used as a **testing base** for new ideas in patient care.

Threats include the continued cutting of **resources**, and **competition** from neighbouring practices which are stealing patients, and hence the capitation fees.

Summary

To summarise, the internal issues are those of human resources management, performance information and measurement, and strategic thinking for the practice as an organisation rather than just a place where individuals dispense care. The external factors include potential funding problems and continued change.

(b) **Introducing change**

Sources of change

(i) **Environmental changes** include the new **funding system**, and the more **competitive approach**.

(ii) **Changes in products and services** include **new medicines** and **therapeutic techniques**, and perhaps a new fashion for **alternative treatments**. The practice seems quite innovative in this respect.

(iii) **Changes in technology and working methods**: conceivably this could include the use of expert systems as diagnostic tools.

(iv) **Changes in management and working relationships**. The appointment of an administrator, over the heads of the existing clerical staff, is an example of this.

(v) **Changes in organisation structure**. This has not yet been mooted, but it is difficult to see how this could be achieved, other than by a shuffling of clerical responsibilities.

Preparing the ground for change. The administrator has to consider the initial **climate of change**. She has to create a culture where innovation and change is desirable.

(i) Ensure that everybody understands what innovation is and how it happens.

(ii) Ensure that the partners accept the need for change.

(iii) Encourage people to think creatively.

(iv) The needs of the various stakeholders must be understood and addressed. It is clear that there has been a communications problem in the past: partners have not explained themselves to staff, who have been working to thwart any change.

(v) Recognise and encourage internal change agents: but in a small practice, the administrator herself is a change agent.

Implementing change. The administrator has to sell change (through reasoned persuasion) rather than command it, because of the limits to her power. A useful model is *Lewin's* unfreeze-change-refreeze model.

(i) The **unfreeze process** can be started by a major event. An example would be the proposed brain-storming session suggested by one of the partners. Senior management are already receptive to change. This could not extend to other members of staff, especially as they will have to be won over eventually. At least there will be the semblance of consultation.

(ii) **Change**. The administrator can suggest that the practice needs a plan, and she can ask for and/or put forward proposals to improve the system of performance measurement employed in the hospital. A well publicised strategic or business plan for the practice, with targets for immunisations etc as well as revenue considerations, can be drawn up. Setting up this system involves disruption and extra effort. If staff, not only the partners, can be told how it benefits them, the change will be easier to implement.

(iii) **Refreeze**. The administrator should ensure the changes are bedded down.

Answer Bank

40 Silvadawn Leisurewear

(a) **Implications of outsourcing to China**

Introduction

Historically, Silvadawn Leisurewear has prided itself in sourcing locally. However, fierce competition has forced the company to revisit their resource purchasing policy and source some of the clothing from manufacturing operations in China. This is seen as a strategic move to remain competitive in the leisurewear market.

Implications

While outsourcing of goods may be thought of as an extension of the normal practice of buying in raw materials, in this case, it is a strategic move to contain the growth of costs. For example, factory hourly **wage rates** in China are 26p an hour (*People Management 2003*). This is a fraction of the UK's minimum wage. This highlights how outsourcing abroad can dramatically reduce the **manufacturing costs** and benefit the Company's overall profit.

However, there is an obvious marketing implication in that eg some **control over the product** offering is surrendered to the supplier and **quality control** can become an issue. Therefore, ways must be found to minimise the likely challenges. One measure to overcome challenges in outsourcing is by briefing.

Briefing an outside supplier is essential, particularly in the case of a dispute. A full brief will leave less room for doubt as to the requirements of the contract. Therefore there must be basic ground rules for briefing. These are:

- To what extent does the Company take outside suppliers into their confidence?
- What does the supplier need to know?
- Who will draw up the briefs?
- How often should the brief be reviewed?

However, **outsourcing arrangements** require **strict attention to contracts**. This can be a source of **operational inflexibility**, if the contract has to be laboriously re-negotiated when circumstances change.

Management of outsourcing requires direct supervision by one or more managers. These managers should also maintain **communication** with the contractors and promote good relations between the parties. If performance is unsatisfactory, the contractor must be informed directly rather than via operational staff so that corrective action is taken. However, **cultural differences** including language could also be an issue. Therefore, the supervising manager needs to be particularly knowledgeable and alert to developments that may affect this relationship. For example, the wage structure of the supplier in China may be below their legislated minimum and will have a direct affect on profitability. However, the Silvadawn Leisurewear is at risk of having their reputable image damaged by accusations of **exploitation** of 'sweatshop' labour.

On the other hand, control rests ultimately with Silvadawn Leisurewear and in particular the quality of the **management control system**. It is vital for quality control that all the goods meet the desired specification and delivered on time. Some mechanisms of control are:

- **Staged payments** – This pays for the goods on arrival. This should be based on targets being met ie quality, agreed delivery dates etc. A proportion of payment should be held back (as agreed in briefing and contract) should contractual obligations not be met.

- **Incentive structure** – In contrast to the above, an incentive scheme can be implemented based on reward for exceeding agreed targets and paid on delivery of goods. However, management must ensure that there is no labour exploitation in an attempt to meet the incentive.

Conclusion

The company must be clear about what it wants to achieve from outsourcing and set **quantifiable standards** against which the contractor's performance can be reviewed. If the outsourcing arrangement goes wrong, the company will not be able to meet their objectives.

(b) **Advantages and disadvantages of moving Call Centre to India**

Introduction

What was once a trickle of UK organisations shifting their call centre operations to the Indian sub-continent, is now becoming a flood. The reason being, India has cornered the Anglophone market by training locals not only in English Language, but also incorporating local English dialects and knowledge. Thus with the problematical developments at Silvadawn's UK based call centre, the Board of Directors is considering re-directing to India.

Advantages

- **Cost** - At present an outsourced Call Centre in the UK can **cost** up to £20 per man hour to run compared with India's £9 (*People Management, 2003*). When international call charges are taken into account, the overall savings can be 40-50% cheaper. Also, there is no capital cost outlay for premises, technology, etc.

- **Culture** – The Indian workforce have been found to be **polite and courteous** and take great pride in being **totally committed** to customer service. For example, finding information out for customers rather than admitting they don't know.

- **Increased profit** – Unit costs could be reduced thus increasing profit and surplus revenue could be **reinvested into the core business** as it is facing fierce competition.

- **Technology** – As this has been a recent innovation within the Indian sub-continent, the technology is considered '**state of the art**'. This will enable immediate information capture from customers ordering via mail order.

- **Management issues** – There will be no further need for a call centre in the UK and **manpower can be reduced**. Along with this, senior management will be able to **focus more time** on core elements of the business rather than being involved with resolving problematic staffing issues previously experienced in the call centre. There will be no need to spend man hours recruiting, selecting and training the desirable 'call centre personality' to do the job.

- **Managing Performance** – The **responsibility** lies with the **outsourced service provider**.

Disadvantages

- **Customers** – Customers may be resistant to calling because they may have the **perception** that a call centre based in India is taking away 'home jobs'.

- **Language** – However much training is given in phonics, accent, dialect etc, **cultural differences** may highlight weaknesses in the delivery of the service eg British humour.

- **Redundancies** – Having to make a number of employees redundant, the cost implication of paying out redundancy packages creates a **cost implication** for the company and could easily damage the good **reputation** and company **image**.

- **Technology** – Even though the majority of call centre technology is 'state of the art', there may still be **variations** in local providers.

- **Political factors** – Although India is a democratic country, there is still **inter-communal tensions** throughout the country. Only recently there was nuclear face off with Pakistan. In the UK, outsourcing to the East has become a politically sensitive issue. This may provide **pressure groups** (including Trade Unions) with 'the ammunition' to instigate boycotts or other action against such organisations.

- **Contingency plans** – As Silvadawn Leisurewear will have little control over the call centre, there must be a **backup service** in operation to ensure that customers' needs are met eg a much reduced centre based in the UK. However, this may not be able to cope with the volume of customer calls and will incur costs for the company.

- **Management issues** – The company prides itself on good customer service however, without **overall control** a problem could develop whereby the good reputation is damaged by poor **customer service**. To ensure this doesn't happen, responsibility and accountability must be given to a company senior manager to oversee this area. In view of this, the manager responsible must have relevant experience and specialist skills (which may not be easy to find) in dealing with the Indian sub-continent. This potentially will involve **further costs** due to **recruitment** of a specialist individual to meet company objectives.

- **Training** – Even though the service provider trains the call centre staff, Silvadawn Leisurewear would still need to make a significant input with regard to **product information training**. It is vital that all staff are fluent and knowledgeable about all the products and services on offer otherwise customers will not return.

- **Control** – **Quality standards need to be met**. However, as the responsibility for recording and monitoring the quality of calls becomes the responsibility of the service provider, it may be necessary for Silvadawn Leisurewear to introduce '**spot checks**' through mystery callers as a means of maintaining those standards. This is likely to incur further costs.

Conclusion

Despite the drawbacks outsourcing to India could be a way to **cut costs** dramatically while simultaneously improving the quality and speed of the operation. However, there are **risks involved** and serious consideration should be given before coming to a decision.

41 CiniCentre

(a) **How stakeholder analysis can assist with formulating vision, objectives and goals.**

   (i) **Stakeholder analysis**

   Conflict - As John reports to a Board of Governors representing most major stakeholders (except employees), he has no alternative but to consider stakeholder interests and the power that they have. Because multiple objectives need to be satisfied and there are potential **conflicts between different stakeholder**

groups, it is not a simple matter. For example, potential conflict can be seen in the example of admission charges. These displease visitors and the tourism industry but are needed to maintain revenue to fund other parts of the organisation.

No dominant stakeholder - In the case of CiniCentre, there is no dominant stakeholder although **some may be more powerful than others**. Central Government, for example is powerful as their grant to the organisation forms the largest contribution to the overall financial revenue however, they exercise their power at 'arms length'. Furthermore, unlike a private company or plc where management is held accountable by shareholders, for any failures, a non-profit organisation such as CiniCentre has no clear line of accountability.

Value of stakeholder analysis – As the planner, John will be forced to look at the environment in a **systematic way**. Analysis of stakeholders' interests and power can inform the vision and mission as well as any **tactical planning**. It also poses some necessary questions about priorities and resources. These will have a significant affect on the vision.

Vision – This is the **desired future state** that the organisation hopes to achieve. Without the views of the various stakeholders, John cannot successfully plan a way forward without a consensus. However, this may be difficult because it may only reveal that different stakeholders have widely differing ideas as to what the centre is all about. Before the 'vision' is finalised, John must convince and gain the support of the Board of Governors.

Mission – This describes why any organisation exists and can direct both its **strategy** and its **guiding values**. The stakeholder analysis **evaluation** can help formulate the reasons for the organisation's existence. For example, Central Government's desire is to maintain the country's heritage for future generations and the general public who want to be entertained with minority interest and classic films.

Agreeing on a mission statement can be a contentious issue however there is no alternative because its **sets strategic direction** for the organisation. A good mission statement should address the concerns of all major stakeholders.

Goals and objectives – These are **related to the existing activities** of the Directorates. From the evaluation of the stakeholder analysis, John will have a much clearer picture of what goals and objectives need to be set. As a result of the findings of the analysis, objectives may now be set to overcome poor quality service and expensive food in the Globe restaurants and other areas for concern. Analysis may also have shown that in this area there are inexperienced staff whose lack of training and expertise is causing poor service. Thus the objective likely to be set is to implement training and development procedures with SMART targets for improving service standards. These objectives can be set right across the board from failure to stay within government financial guidelines to improving labour relations within the organisation. All of which will benefit from the analysis.

However, **stakeholders** will exercise **constraints** over what is achievable. A business plan under these circumstances could not ride 'roughshod' over the variety of stakeholder views because of the power of certain pressure groups and their influence within the media. For example, they may well persuade CiniCentre to modify their plans.

Answer Bank

(ii) **Main stakeholder groups**

The following four stakeholders have been identified.

Members of the Centre – People join societies such as the CiniCentre for a **variety** of reasons. Some may be more **active** than others (eg putting themselves up for election) and some may simply be pursuing a **vague interest** in films and are chiefly interested in the publications and discounts that membership can bring. Members have **little power** as individuals unless they are distinguished film-makers, producers or actors. Although members are able to exercise voice through their representatives on the Board of Governors (particularly at election time) the power is probably latent rather than active for the individual.

Employees and management - Their interest is in **continued employment** and the continued **interest of the job**. Obviously they must love film, particularly in the Film Archive Unit, where specialist expertise is highly valued. Staff in the museum must also enjoy their work and have good interpersonal skills as they deal with the public whose expectations of quality rise. In the **short-term** staff have the **power to disrupt** totally the operations (strike) of the CiniCentre however in the long-term these actions may be self-defeating. On the other hand the staff at the FAU have little power in the short-term other than resignation, but they **could do long-term damage** to the CiniCentre's reputation and mission. As a manager John has significant executive power, but less than he probably had in his previous job.

Central government – As a **public venture**, should the funds be withdrawn, there would be a major protest especially from the media were the Cinicentre to close. It is a tourist attraction in London, **provides jobs, supports education** and is prestigious for Britain. They exercise the **largest** of the **stakeholder powers** and also provides most of the CiniCentre's revenue, covering most of its overheads.

Media – British media firms may see the CiniCentre as a **resource for programming ideas**. The film industry, for example, will be keen to **promote and interest in the cinema**, both as an art and as entertainment. The media has **no direct power** as they contribute no income other than fees for the use of films from archives. Nonetheless they are powerful as they **can mobilise the attention and interest of the public**.

(b) **Briefing Paper: Process of strategic management**

Introduction

It is proposed that a model of **formal strategic planning and management** is introduced. It has the following characteristics.

- A logical sequence of analysis, choice, evaluation and implementation
- Clear objectives that the strategies must support for the long and short-term
- Direction by and large by senior management
- Strategies are chosen after an objective evaluation of the facts
- Strategic decisions cover the scope of the organisation's activities, its position in the environment and its general direction

Although there are other approaches this rational model is perhaps the most suited at the current time.

Process of strategic management

Below is the systematic process.

- **Strategic analysis** – In this process the mission and objectives are set first. In the case of CiniCentre there is no current mission or vision but these should be developed after a more fundamental strategic review.

- **Environmental analysis** – This is a key issue given the multiplicity of stakeholders and its ability to secure revenue in the future. This takes account of the following factors:

    - **Political** – Government and Local Authority grants are set every year. The government however may have other priorities and see the CiniCentre as a waste of money. Therefore, there is a need to cultivate friends of the charity in all political parties, government departments, media and sport.

    - **Economic** – These determine people's prosperity and their willingness and ability to spend on discretionary items such as subscriptions and donations. In prosperous times leisure spending increases and as admission charges and catering account for over 50% of revenue this is important.

    - **Social and cultural factors** – Visitors and members have many other calls on their leisure time. An analysis of social and cultural trends can help predict future income from admission or suggest marketing approaches to increasing admissions. It might also suggest means of segmentation. The CineCentre appears at the moment to be alienating its target audience. This is all the more surprising as cinema admissions in the UK have been rising for a number of years.

    - **Technology** – New management information systems may be an essential constituent of strategic control as well as the huge growth in the e-commerce industry. Also, the CineCentre is influenced by the changes in the technology of displaying and distributing the moving image.

- **Internal audit** – This can highlight strengths and weaknesses within the organisation eg if FAU fail to meet appropriate standards this might lead to a re-direction of government funding. The audit will identify CineCentre's current resources and operations and see if they are applied efficiently and effectively. It will also highlight pressures for eg salary demands, maintenance costs and equipment.

- **Strategic options generation** – Deals with products/services and markets. This is followed by **evaluation** where alternative strategies are developed and each is then examined on its merits. These are:

    - Acceptability to the organisation's stakeholders
    - Suitability
    - Feasibility

    This is followed by **selection** from the following:

    - Competitive strategy is the generic strategy determining how you compete.
    - Product-market strategy determines where you compete.
    - Institutional strategies determine the method of grown.

    All of the above need to be carefully considered by John before he embarks on his strategic approach.

- **Evaluation and control** – Once the plan has been implemented it can be evaluated by the actual performance against **established standards**. This can be followed with taking **corrective action** as necessary.

The benefits of the strategic management approach is that it will force the Governors to take a **long-term view** of the CineCentre, agree with what it is for, establish priorities and play to its strengths. Not least, it will present them with a strategy for containing and hopefully reducing accumulated deficit.

(c) **Strategic control**

An approach to strategic control that uses a variety of performance indicators is *Kaplan and Norton's* balanced scorecard. This typically involves identifying performance on the basis of four perspectives.

(i) **Customer perspective** – Customers can be defined broadly in this context to include internal customers and stakeholders.

(ii) **Internal business perspective** – This covers the business processes that have greatest impact on customer satisfaction.

(iii) **Innovation and learning perspective** – How far current and future needs are taken into account; employee motivation and learning.

(iv) **Financial perspective** – Return on capital, cash flow. This presupposes that the current financial information is of any use eg there are major flaws, in particular, the way that overheads are treated in the CineCentre's management accounts.

The balanced scorecard does not de-value budgeting but shows the linkages between different areas of the budget for its long-term strategic health. In CineCentre's case the financial perspective has perhaps been inappropriately managed. With this approach, objectives from departments and business units can be integrated with financial performance.

This method of performance measurement was developed for business, however, it can be adapted to the particular circumstances of CineCentre. The internal business perspective can be adopted to improve the admission of the centre eg ticketing if this is a problem area. It can also be used to address the procedures in the FAU that deal with chemically unstable material. The customer perspective can be tackled by admissions, repeat admissions, memberships subscriptions and participation as well as market research. It is also a means of warning against short-termist cost cutting, as it exposes the hidden costs eg falling number of admissions in making savings.

- **Performance Measures** – (Film Archive Unit)

    (i) **Operating measures** – The number of films saved, number of films destroyed, alternatively footage of films saved/destroyed, sponsorship income, the ability to reach government standards and publications.

    (ii) **Financial measures** – Efficiency (eg building costs, administration etc), revenue.

    (iii) **Conservation** – This is a long-term effort but some simple measures (eg number of films saved) are appropriate. However, objectives might be set in terms of publicity, project planning and management. This ensures that this programme is conducted efficiently and effectively, but clearly the financial perspective is not much use other than for overall cost control.

42 Paperworks plc

(a) **Increasing innovation**

To: James Bell, Managing Director
From: Gemma Lawrence, Marketing Consultant
Subject: Innovation
Date: 11th June 20X0

1.0 Introduction

Innovation is an organisation's ability to create and implement new services, new products and new ways of doing business. The chief objective of innovation is to ensure the organisation's **survival** and **success** in a **changing world**. Being innovative allows the development of prompt and imaginative **solutions** to problems (through the use of project teams) and can generate greater **confidence** inside and outside the organisation in its ability to cope with change.

2.0 Innovation Audit

The innovation audit is a process that examines whether the necessary assets and competencies are present in an organisation. These can be examined through four key areas.

- The current **organisational climate with regard to innovation**. *Burnside* suggests there are eight influential factors that support innovation and four areas that act as **constraints** eg resources. These **support** innovation by the amount of access to appropriate resources in terms of facilities, staff, finance and information. Insufficient time, for example, would act as a constraint as there would be no time to consider alternative approaches to under take the work. Another important factor is the use of **metaphors** to describe the organisation eg this organisation is like a super tanker, it takes a long time to change direction.

- Hard measures of the organisation's **current performance in innovation**. These may include: the rate of new product development in the last three years, customer satisfaction rating across all areas of customer service, staff turnover and a **innovation value portfolio analysis** which looks at the strategic business units or products to establish whether they are 'settlers', 'migrators' or 'pioneers'.

- Review of the organisation's **policies and practices** that are currently **used to support innovation**. These will look at the **structures or procedures** already in place that have been developed to try and facilitate creativity and innovation

- It is important to have a **balance of cognitive styles** within the senior management team. The nature of innovation demands a variety to ensure development of creative ideas. If all managers had the same style, this could act as a constraint on innovation.

3.0 Reasons for lack of innovation

A key benefit of a marketing audit is to identify reasons for the lack of innovation within an organisation. In the case of Paperworks, it would appear that the organisation has a strong product research and development (R&D) programme. While there is evidence of a wider lack of innovation there is some to suggest a degree of product innovation. However, this is not always linked to market needs. The reasons for lack of innovation may also include:

- Ineffective organisational structure - This can restrict innovation.
- Lack of investment in R&D and training.
- Poor marketing orientation - Not placing the customer at the centre.
- Lack of communication - Particularly between inside and outside project teams.
- Poor internal marketing - No obvious internal marketing process in place.
- Aversion to risks - Emphasis on sticking to traditional ways of doing things.
- Internal politics - People with vested interests may not support others creative or innovative ideas.

4.0 **Increasing the pace of innovation**

With an understanding of the reasons for the lack of innovation, recommendations can be made for increasing the pace of innovation. This could be done in two stages. In the first instance, the organisation's culture needs to be addressed and secondly, there is a need to speed up the new product development (NPD) process. It is recommended that:

- **The creativity infrastructure is addressed**. Senior management must **support** and **encourage** creativity and the structures necessary for developing creative ideas.
- **Recognition** be given to innovative ideas and a **reward** system linked to business performance is in place.
- Individuals have sufficient **freedom** to control their work and ideas.
- There is a **collaborative and co-operative atmosphere** where all individuals have a **shared vision** of the organisation.
- The level of **commitment** to the current work within a team situation is based on **trust** and **willingness** to help each other.
- **Customers are involved** in the evaluation process of new products before launch.
- **Parallel processing** takes place where activities are undertaken concurrently.
- There are **multi-functional teams** that provide a range of expertise needed to develop and launch new products.
- **Knowledge management** is used to promote continuous innovation. This can be defined as 'any process or practice of creating, acquiring, capturing, sharing and using knowledge, wherever it resides, to enhance learning and performance in organisations' (*Scarborough and Swan*).

(b) **Internet development**

Introduction

As the recent internal review highlighted, Paperworks' website is ineffective and is currently little more than an online brochure. This is in stark contrast to the major competitor Universal Paper, who has a highly sophisticated website that enables customers to request samples, view current samples and place and track orders. In order to keep abreast with competition, Paperworks will need to transform their online capability.

(i) **Improving online capability**

Owing to the newness of the Internet, few companies have a clearly **defined strategy** for their website. If a site is developed without clearly defined strategic goals it will not be possible to identify how successful it is. Only through setting **realistic goals** and then assessing whether they are achieved, can an organisation be sure of the contribution Internet-based marketing is making. Therefore to improve online capability, Paperworks must develop an **Internet marketing strategy** as outlined by Chaffey *et al's* simple framework shown below.

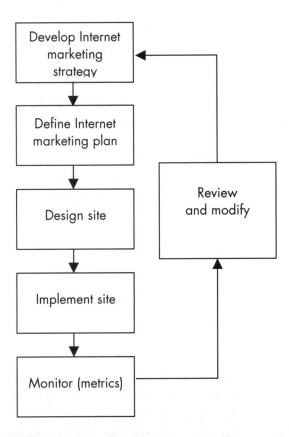

A simple framework for Internet marketing strategy development

As shown above, there is a **natural progression** for developing the website for **supporting marketing activities**. This progression starts at:

- **Level 0** – No website.

- **Level 1** – The organisation places an entry in a website that lists company name eg Yellow Pages. There is no website at this stage.

- **Level 2** – Simple static website containing basic organisational and product information is created (brochureware).

- **Level 3** – Simple interactive site where users are able to search and make queries to retrieve information on product availability and pricing. Queries by e-mail may also be supported.

- **Level 4** – Interactive site supporting transactions with users.

- **Level 5** – Fully interactive site providing relationship marketing with individual customers and facilitating the full range of marketing functions.

At present Paperworks is at Level 2 only providing brochureware ie displaying their brochure online. Therefore, to remain **competitive**, particularly against Universal Paper, there is an urgency to develop the site to Level 5. However, this must be part of the **strategic business plan** and not developed in isolation.

With the assumption that building the website is an **integral part** of the marketing strategy, the following points outlined below must be taken into account.

- There needs to be **sufficient investment** (monetarily and resources) plus the management and staff to be committed to the project.
- **Marketing research** to answer the following questions:
    - What are the key audiences for the site?
    - What should the content of site be?
    - Which customer service capabilities will the organisation provide for customers? eg integrating an extranet to support existing customers.
    - How will the site be structured?
    - How will navigation around the site occur?
- Once **analysis** has determined the information needs of the site, it can then be designed. The **design** is critical to the success of the website as customers will not return if they have a negative experience. Research has shown that the most common reasons for return are: high quality content; ease of use; quick to download and updated frequently.

Implementation of the above will dramatically improve Paperworks online capability and enable it to remain at the cutting edge.

(ii) **Monitoring effectiveness**

Chaffey *et al* suggest that to measure effectiveness of Internet marketing, three different techniques can be applied. These are:

- **Business effectiveness measures** – These **assess** how the Internet is affecting the **performance** of the whole business ie what impact the Internet has on the business. These are general **financial measures** and include some of the following:
    - Direct online contribution to revenue.
    - Indirect online contribution to revenue.
    - Profitability of website ie the direct revenue of the website minus the operational costs of the site.
    - Return on investments (ROI). This is a measurement over a longer period that calculates the return (amount of revenue) compared with the initial investment and operational costs.
    - Operational cost reductions. For example, Sysko estimate that their web site has saved the business over 20% of its operational costs as compared with not having the site.

As well as assessing financial measures, business effectiveness measures should access whether the specific corporate objectives for the website defined in the strategic plan have been achieved.

- **Marketing effectiveness measures** – These will reflect how well the web site is fulfilling the needs of the marketing manager. These will be more **traditional marketing measures** and will include some of the following:
    - Customer acquisition on new leads generated
    - Sales generated directly and indirectly
    - Impact on market penetration and demand
    - Customer satisfaction and retention rates of clients who use the Internet, compared with those who do not
    - Incremental or cross sales achieved through the Internet
    - Impact of Internet on customer satisfaction, loyalty and brand
    - Internet sales as a proportion of all sales made by the organisation compared with all sales in the market.

    As well as being interested in measures related to marketing outcomes, the marketing manager would like to know how much the website is helping to reduce costs. For example, reduction in costs of promotional material; cost of acquiring a new customer and the cost of developing/supporting an existing customer relationship through time.

- **Internet marketing effectiveness** – This involves **assessing** how well the particular **online techniques** are working. Some of these are:
    - **Capture** – How affected is the organisation in attracting customers to the site using online and offline promotional methods? Does the site use banner advertisements, offline advertisements with specific URLs? Does it use search engine meta-tags? How well do these work?
    - **Content** – How well are customers supported with information and ease of use through the content and design of the site? The speed and availability of the site? Is the online proposition clear?
    - **Customer orientation** – Does the content suit its target audience ie in job specific, industry specific or country specific terms? Is it easy for a particular audience to find information? Is it relevant, accurate, up-to-date? How well are clients supported at different stages of the buying decision? What incentives are there for clients to return to the site at each stage?
    - **Community and interactivity** – How well are the customer needs met as an individual by providing community facilities and establishing an interactive dialogue?

    Online metrics enable marketers to build a picture of which parts of their web sites are working well and which are not.

(iii) **Privacy and Data Protection**

In recent years there has been a growing fear that the every increasing amount of information about individuals held by organisations could be misused. In particular, an individual could easily be harmed by the existence of computerised data about him or her that was **inaccurate or misleading** and which could be transferred to unauthorised third parties at high speed and little cost.

The **Data Protection Act 1998** is an attempt to protect the individual. There terms of the Act cover data about individuals - not data about corporate bodies. The Act has two main aims.

- To **protect individual privacy**. Previous UK law only applied to computer based information. The 1988 Act applies to all personal data in any form.

- To **harmonise data protection legislation** so that in the interest of improving the operation of the single European market, there can be a free flow of personal data between the member states of the EU.

The Data Protection Registrar keeps a **registration of all data users**. Only registered data users are permitted to hold personal data. The data user must only hold data and use data for the registered purposes.

The Act establishes the following rights for data subjects.

- The data subject may seek **compensation** through the Courts for damage and any associated distress caused by the loss, **destruction or unauthorised disclosure** of data about himself or herself or by inaccurate data about himself or herself.

- The subject may obtain **access** to personal data of which he or she is the subject and apply to the Courts for any **inaccurate** data to be put right or to be wiped off the data users files.

- The subject can **sue** a data user for any **damage or distress** caused by incorrect or misleading data.

- Everyone has the right to go to Court to seek redress for any **breach of data** protection law.

43 Selfridges

(a) **Effective leadership**

Whereas management focuses on co-ordination eg day-to-day administration; organising structures; establishing systems; control etc, leadership is concerned with influencing the performance of individuals and groups and motivating and inspiring them to higher levels of performance and being an innovative thinker. Both sets of skills and activities are essential however current thinking suggests there are links between leadership and innovative thinking. This said be the determining factor in the success of any organisation (*Needle*).

Leadership lies at the heart of management in that managers can only get the job done through other people. In this way, *John Adair* sees leadership in terms of the interaction of:

- Achieving the task
- Building the team
- Developing the individual

To Adair these three factors are the essence of leadership and no one element can be achieved without the other as shown in the table below.

Key action	Task	Team	Individuals
Define objectives	Identify job that needs doing and the constraints you have to work with	Involve team in project and get them committed	Make sure they understand and accept the objectives
Plan	Establish priorities, check resources, decide and set standards and procedure	Consult the team, encouraging ideas and building on their suggestions	Assess skills and experience. Set individual targets and delegate
Brief	Brief the team and check understanding	Answer questions and obtain feedback	Listen to ideas and be enthusiastic about their contributions
Support and monitor	Access progress and maintain quality standards and discipline	Co-ordinate their efforts and reconcile their conflicts	Advise and counsel, assist and reassure, recognise individual effort
Evaluate	Summarise what has been achieved. Review objectives and re-plan if necessary	Recognise and celebrate. Learn from failure	Assess performance, appraise progress and guide and train

In my opinion new leadership at Selfridges exemplifies Adair's model above.

- **Task** – New leadership has brought a **clear vision of the future**. **Building on the vision of the founder**, with past experience, impartiality and fresh ideas, clear leadership has brought continued positive behaviour change and clarity about the values of the organisation. A **radical change process** was initiated with refurbishment of the London store. The **stated aim** was to implement **brand focused retailing** and make Selfridges 'a store of the next century'.

- **Team** - Old ways of working were questioned and a **change to the structure** of the organisation has taken place. For example, there are **now five functional directors** who report to the CEO. Each has his or her own staff of senior managers. Business managers report to each of the general managers of the stores. Business managers in return, are responsible for sales managers, each of whom is responsible for one or more departments. There is now **responsibility** and **accountability in identifiable roles with no duplication**. The **new Selfridges style** is contemporary reflecting the **'spirit of the city'** and there is no longer a struggle between old and new.

  - **Individuals** – **Culture surveys** were conducted, **focus groups** were organised and the old job evaluation scheme was replaced with a **broadbanding pay arrangement**. Great emphasis has been put on **training and development** with a new emphasis on a **coaching** approach to help staff learn from their experiences in contrast to traditional teaching and training. The directors sponsor the

management development programmes and managers, in turn, learn how to develop their staff. **Individuals are listened to** and action taken eg the Board asked team leaders to re-apply for their jobs after negative feedback after the first survey. **Individual appraisals** are also undertaken where praise is given (**recognition**) and even small gifts (**rewards**).

By identifying the **task** ie the vision to become 'a store of the next century', the **team** were involved and committed to the vision and **individuals** understood and accepted the objectives. This effective leadership has enabled Selfridges to transform into 'a store of the 21st Century'.

Leadership qualities

In today's business climate it is necessary for people and organisations to continue to adapt if they are going to survive long into the 21st Century. *Schermerhorn* states that at the very least a 21st Century leader must be a:

- **Global strategist** – Understanding the interconnections amongst nations, cultures and economies; planning and acting with due consideration.

- **Master of technology** – Comfortable with information technology; understanding technological trends and implications; able to use technology to best advantage.

- **Inspiring leader** – Attracting highly motivated workers and inspiring them with a high performance culture where individuals and teams can do their best work.

- **Model of ethical behaviour** – Acting ethically in all ways, setting high ethical standards for others to follow, building a work culture that values ethics and social responsibility.

Linking the above to the case study, it can be assumed that the CEO is a global strategist because the company has historically been involved in international enterprise ie part of the Sears retailing empire in the USA. He will be **astute and knowledge** about eg possible threats from overseas competitors in terms of takeover bids, competition etc.

He must have a good understanding of the latest **systems and operations management** technology thus, enabling the managers to be up to the minute with financial, stock and customer information.

The leader will need to continue to motivate and inspire employees to **meet company objectives** and **shareholder expectations**. For example, figures at the end of the two-year survey indicate that sales were up 23% on the previous year, costs were 5% down and contribution is 32% up. This new enhanced **reputation** will further attract highly motivated individuals with a desire for high performance to work with a **committed**, **harmonious** and **efficient team**.

By setting out a **Values Matrix for stakeholders** eg community, customer, shareholder, suppliers and employees, the CEO is clearly building and defining a work culture that values **ethics and social responsibility**. For example, ensuring from the employee point of view it is a friendly and welcoming place to work and, a project like 'the spirit of the city' highlights the **community value** where managers and staff get involved in a range of **community projects**.

(b) **Factors affecting the organisation**

External factors

- **Political** – Government policy affects the whole economy, and governments are responsible for enforcing and creating a **stable framework** in which business can be done. However, the political environment is not simply limited to legal factors. Daily media suggests we live in an **era of constant change**, political instability, international terrorism and a resurgence of **world conflict** that affects the economy of the world and ultimately an individual's sense of security and stability.

- **Economic** - As a result of the **competitive global developments** leading to increasing marginality, new markets have to be continuously sought and created. Selfridges therefore face constant changes to their business environment. **Exchange rates** impact on the cost of imports, selling prices and cost of hedging against fluctuations. This ultimately affects the economic **growth** of the organisation and their capital, flow and trade. This rapidly **changing market environment** can, however, be of benefit to Selfridges in that it is an opportunity to sustain competitive advantage through the principal of *Kaizan*, ie to stay at the cutting edge of the market, continuous improvement is a necessary requirement for the organisation.

- **Social** – The CIM/Henley Centre report, *'Metamorphosis in Marketing'* details how **consumer behaviour and attitudes are changing**. The growth in 'minority' lifestyles is creating opportunities for niche brands aimed at consumers with very distinct purchasing habits. There are continuously **changing fashions and trends**. Globalisation has brought about a **question of conscience**. The information revolution and telecommunication infrastructure has increased **customer awareness** of irresponsible marketing, political activities and environmental, animal and human rights issues. The ease of modern transportation encourages international business and people to travel, which has ultimately **educated** and **enlightened** individuals to the world around them. Along with the **sectoral shift from manufacturing to the service industry** in the UK in the latter part of the 20th Century has come a reduction in Trade Union power putting more **power back in the hands of management**.

- **Technological** – Innovation is bringing the ability to create large numbers of product variants without corresponding increases in resources. This is causing markets to become overcrowded. The fragmentation of the media to service ever more specialist and local audiences is denying mass media the ability to assure market dominance for major brand advertisers. This creates space for niche players and speeds up the diffusion of **innovation thus shortening life cycles**. The advance in information technology is enabling information about individual customers to be organised in ways that enable highly selective and personal communications. It also fuels **quicker 'me-too'** product launches that potentially shorten product life cycles.

- **Environmental** - For many people being 'green' is paramount. Selfridges will be forced to respond to **ethical consumerism** by practising good ethics and having to publish codes of practice. It is considered an ethical matter today as well as an astute purchasing decision for consumers to reward only those organisations that have a good record for selling quality products, honour guarantees, exchange faulty goods and to avoid known offenders.

- **Legal** – Selfridges are obligated to conform to EU and Parliamentary legislation and regulation. For example, there is a general legal framework where there is a basic way of doing business. This framework consists of eg company law, employment law, health and safety, marketing and sales etc.

Internal Factors

There is a need for **clear vision** of the future of brand focused retailing, **clear leadership** and **continued behaviour change** linked to a clarity about the values of the organisation.

Selfridges must continuously seek opportunities for improvement through a systematic **process of development**. This should include looking at **core competences** of the organisation, **capabilities** of individuals and teams and performance management.

Effective positioning in the mind of the customer is critical to brand success. Therefore, to increase profitability **customer behaviour and motivation should be understood** while building on product experience and marketing initiatives and associating the organisation's trademark with compelling **customer values**. It would appear Selfridges take this one step further by offering a sense of 'community' amidst creativity and an approach to make the shopping experience more fun and entertaining which is appealing to customers and staff alike.

While the concept of turning the values of stakeholders into **value in terms of business success** is promoted, the values expressed to the outside world are reflected internally. The core values of Friendly, Aspirational, Accessible and Bold give Selfridges its point of difference as employees, customers and suppliers are all treated in the same respectful way.

There is a **need to develop** through sharing knowledge, experiencing local culture, reflecting and learning from the experience. As Selfridges' focus is on the 'customers wants and needs', it is apparent that there is a need to develop a **shared value** with the customer while providing them with an **enjoyable shopping experience** with offerings of all that is fashionable and desirable and ultimately an **image with which to identify**.

The prevailing traditional **culture** was well entrenched and transformation will have brought about mixed reactions amongst staff. It is human nature to go through transitional phases in the **process of change**. For some it is seen as an ending, neutral zone phase and a new beginning (Bridges). For others, change may come as a shock and go through a process of denial, depression, letting go, acceptance of reality, testing, consolidation, internalisation, reflection and learning over a period of time (Hayes).

It can be argued that Selfridges' **success is dependent on the ability to share values** across the organisation in such a way as to achieve their vision. There is a need to be **proactive** and one step ahead of competitors, **flexible** and **geared to an internal environment** in order to sustain a competitive advantage.

Building on the central structural changes to accommodate the CEO's vision of Selfridges being the 'House of Brands' it is suggested that consideration should be given to the concept of '**selling responsibility**'.

44 Woodstock Furniture

> *Examiner's comments.* The compulsory question will be used to challenge students about strategic marketing communications issues. The following terms should be highlighted in this context.
>
> - Positioning
> - Differentiation
> - Added value
> - Strategic approaches (pull, push, profile)
> - Resources (especially financial)
> - Objectives
> - Audience
> - Message style
> - Media selection
> - Integration
>
> The majority of students used a suitable framework, but were unable to develop strategy or consider Woodstock's corporate brand. Another disappointing feature was the poor use of the figures that had been provided.

Integrated Marketing Communications Plan

for

Woodstock Furniture Co Ltd

Prepared by

A CIM Student
June 20X0

Executive summary

This marketing communications plan for Woodstock Furniture Company seeks to build on the business and marketing strategies and over the next two years develop the Woodstock corporate brand. Funds are limited and this plan seeks to develop the brand by **repositioning** it away from the high street competitors as a high quality craftsman brand. This will be achieved by making the brand aspirational and will use a range of promotional tools designed to reinforce the craftsman position and by stimulating word-of-mouth communications.

> **Contents**
>
> **Executive Summary**
>
> **Introduction**
>
> **Context Analysis**
>
> **Promotional Goals**
>
> **Marketing Communications Strategy**
>
> **Promotional Methods**
>
> **Budget and Management Control**
>
> **Evaluation**

Introduction

This Integrated Marketing Communications (IMC) plan has been developed for the Woodstock Furniture Co (WFC) based on the information provided in the briefing document. It covers a two year period and is designed to **build on the marketing strategy** which has already been put into position. WFC needs to develop its corporate brand and this plan sets out the way in which this is to be achieved, the costs and the timing associated with the activities.

Context analysis

In order to understand the situation facing WFC it is necessary to understand the context within which the communications are to be implemented. The following analysis sets out some of the key communications related issues facing the company.

Business context

The company's performance has been quite variable over the past few years. Revenue has grown to £1.7m and profits stand at £117,300. Market share is 21% and the corporate goal is to grow at 15% pa. This may be difficult in a static market but with property prices in London and the South East starting to level out more people may decide to withdraw their homes from the market and wait for prices to rise in the future. In the meantime they may choose to refurbish their kitchens. Kitchens are an important room for buyers when they consider a house purchase.

The competition from the high street brands is seen as a threat but in terms of materials, product quality and design they do not attract the more discerning customer, sought by WFC. The **promotional materials** used by these large brands pose a threat and serve to homogenise the market. As a result of this there has been a change to the organisation's view of its own business. It no longer perceives itself as a manufacturer and installer but as a craftsman based company who design and construct high quality furniture to match and complement the interior of a home. This decision represents a repositioning away from the high street retailer based competition and seeks to differentiate the Woodstock brand. This change in purpose needs to be communicated to relevant stakeholders and acts as the base for this communications plan.

Customer context

WFC customers are characterised by their wealth. They are **affluent** and can afford to have kitchens and bathrooms crafted to complement their homes. It is important to them that they appoint companies who attend to detail and who are able to match the decor of their homes. The communications that are recommended here reflect the privacy that the target audience values. The purchase decision represents **high involvement** so it is important to develop positive attitudes prior to purchase. This will require the **development of high levels of trust** which needs to be converted into commitment to the WFC brand. The strength of the credibility and subsequent customer satisfaction with their new installation should help provoke positive word of mouth comment. Advocacy can be developed if post purchase communications maintain levels of purchase satisfaction and privacy.

Members of the target market take pride in their homes and have a **modern outlook**. This is demonstrated by their interest in new technology and innovations generally. It should therefore be quite feasible to communicate with them through the Internet.

The marketing plan specifies that **alliances** are to be **created** with **other manufacturers** in related markets (conservatories, studies) which represent a horizontal dimension. In addition, new markets are to be approached through the development of new relationships with architects and property developers in what is a vertical dimension. This will require suitable communications.

Stakeholders

The brief fails to mention other stakeholders in detail but WFC needs to **identify key stakeholder audiences**. These may be associated with the new markets (eg trading association for conservatory manufacturers) or financial institutions and venture capitalists in an attempt to attract investment. Communications with these audiences need to reflect the values and performance of WFC rather than product range or terms of business.

Organisational context

The company needs to **update its old systems** and procedures and become more efficient. However, the values associated with craftsmanship must not be lost. Rather, they need to be incorporated in the style and format of communications with the various target audiences. One way of doing this is to **build** on the **loyalty** and **affinity** many of the staff have for the organisation. Their knowledge of the market and the organisation can be used to signal high value, prestige and their behaviour harnessed as a strong corporate identity cue.

One of the most critical factors is the small amount of financial resources available for marketing communications.

External context

The wider external environment is relatively unimportant in this context. It is unlikely that changes in the political arena will impact on the company but **changes in the economic conditions** (eg changes in capital gains taxation, stamp duty) might affect decisions to invest in kitchen furniture. However, it is felt that promotional materials and the new position should not stress, or even mention price, as this is not a decision criteria for this target audience. Wider social influences are few and technological influences limited to the methods WFC can use to communicate with its target audiences.

Promotional goals

Three main types of objective can be determined:

(a) **Corporate objectives**

These refer to the revised mission which repositions the organisation as a craftsman based organisation which designs and builds high quality bespoke furniture. This needs to be understood and accepted by all employees within 3 months and 75% of all strategically significant stakeholders within 6 months.

(b) **Marketing objectives**

These are that the company must grow at 15% per annum, that prices should be adjusted to reflect the premium position and that new marketing channels (vertical and horizontal based relationships) need to be developed.

(c) **Marketing communication objectives**

The marketing communication objectives are to reposition the company and develop a corporate brand which reflects values of craftsmanship.

In order to accomplish this it will be necessary first to **raise awareness** (60% prompted) amongst the target customer audiences, then build positive attitudes towards the brand. This will be accomplished over the next two years.

In addition, communications need to reach architects and property developers (80% awareness) and links with other carefully selected manufacturers need to be established.

Marketing communications strategy

Owning a WFC kitchen should be regarded as a **signal of achievement**. However, the limited amount of funding restricts the amount and impact that the marketing communications can be expected to deliver. Therefore, a strong pull strategy is not realistic at this stage of development. The main weight of the campaign should be directed to a **profile strategy** and the generation of word of mouth communications. The essence of the profile strategy is to differentiate WFC on the basis of its total craft approach, employee skills and overall attention to the detail of customer needs. The brand needs to be repositioned as **aspirational** among successful entrepreneurs, sports personalities and other celebrities.

The strategy should be built first around the employees. These people need to be trained in **customer service** and **management** so that they carry and reflect the high values of the WFC brand. Whilst this is proceeding we need to reconsider the design elements of our corporate identity to ensure that it conveys the correct values that support the Woodstock brand, in all the ways that we project it (letterhead, workwear, vehicles etc).

The next stage will involve the **development** of a **suitable web site** that seeks to provide information and be capable of collecting information about potential customers. A more extensive and interactive web site will be beyond the current resource levels and should be developed as a separate business strategy, at a later date.

A **suitable set of consistent corporate identity cues** need to be developed and conveyed through reasonable points of contact with customers and architects.

In order to reach architects and other specifiers a **push strategy** is also required. This includes appropriate sales literature which must include product specification (capabilities) information. High quality photography is not important, just the accuracy and completeness of the information provided.

Towards the end of the two year period aspects of a pull strategy might be introduced.

Promotional methods

In order for the corporate brand to become established, a **word of mouth** campaign is to be developed, perhaps through a viral email campaign and selected kitchen based 'parties' (events) at special high profile locations.

Public relations activities are essential and could feed off the 'parties' by placing articles and editorial features about kitchens and related issues, in suitable magazines and newspapers. This is crucial to establish the values of the WFC brand.

Advertising in trade journals will be necessary during the first year. Placement in up-market consumer magazines is recommended towards the end of year 2 or possibly later as the word of mouth campaign may still be running.

Sponsorship may not be possible but should be considered for the longer term. An association with the arts, certain food manufacturers or fashionable yet well designed restaurants may complement the required positioning.

Personal selling remains an important part of the promotional mix. This is necessary not only to finalise customer orders but also to meet architects and to arrange horizontal alliances. In reality, there may only be a few people in the organisation responsible for personal selling but regardless of their status, these people need to be advised of the repositioning, given suitable promotional materials and trained in closing orders to increase the conversion ratio. Selling to architects and specifiers is very different to selling to end user customers. It may be worth considering the recruitment of someone with suitable skills and experience which can then be transferred internally.

Direct marketing will be useful in the second year as names and addresses of potential customers build. The current format of the brochure needs to be revised especially with the technical data required by the specifiers. The craft approach needs to be reflected in a contemporary style.

It is important that these activities be coordinated, timed and delivered in such a way that the audience perceives a single consistent message, whether this be through the actions of employees or through the web site or sales brochures.

Budget and management control

The budget available to WFC is approximately £85,000 for each of the two years of the campaign. This represents 5% of revenue and does not take into account higher margins or increased revenue in year 2. Cash flow needs to be monitored carefully to ensure there is no over commitment to the marketing communications strategy.

PROMOTIONAL TOOL	Q1	Q2	Q3	Q4	Q5	Q6	Q7	Q8
Public Relations	x	X		x	x	x		x
Email Campaign			x	x				
Direct Marketing						x	x	x
Advertising – Consumer								x
Advertising – Trade				x	x	x		
Employee Training & Communications	x	X			x			x
PROMOTIONAL TOOL	Q1	Q2	Q3	Q4	Q5	Q6	Q7	Q8
Corporate Literature and Sales Brochures		X				x		
Web Site Development	x	X	x					

Table Schedule of Promotional Methods

Evaluation

The campaign should be evaluated not only at the end but also periodically through the campaign's life. The limited number of funds suggests that official recall and recognition techniques will not be possible. However, it should be possible to record informally where and how new customers and architects first heard of WFC. Once the Web Site is up the number of hits and the collection of names, addresses and other materials should be possible.

Finally, the campaign should be tracked against the objectives listed above. It is through some understanding of the level of awareness and the attitudes held about the Woodstock brand that the true worth of the campaign will be understood.

45 Campaigns of global pressure

(a) To: The Director, Polmer Products plc
    From: Jeff Winn, Management Consultant
    Subject: Campaigns of Global Pressure
    Date: 20th June 20X2

In response to your request, the following report addresses your outlined concerns.

1.0 **Corporate social responsibility**

The European Commission defines corporate **social responsibility** (CSR) as 'a concept whereby **companies integrate social and environmental concerns** in their business operations and in their interaction with their stakeholders on a voluntary basis'. The CSR agenda has evolved to include how businesses deliver on employment policies, community investment, diversity, customer relations, training and recruitment practices, as key stakeholder concerns. There is also a move to incorporate disabled stakeholders within the confines of CSR.

Businesses, particularly large ones, are subject to increasing expectations that they will exercise social responsibility. This is an ill defined concept, but appears to focus on the provision of specific benefits to society in general, such as charitable donations, the creation or preservation of employment, and spending on environmental improvement or maintenance. A great deal of the pressure is created by the activity of minority action groups and is aimed at businesses because they are perceived to possess extensive resources.

As highlighted in the case study, 9 out of 10 people in the Mori survey take CSR into account when making a purchasing decision, and 7 out of 10 people think that business does not pay enough attention to social responsibility. This creates a compelling argument for companies to develop **policies** that incorporate addressing the issue of CSR. As 90% of customers take CSR into account during their decision-making process to purchase goods or services, it seems to makes good sense to adopt policies as a source of competitive advantage. The Co-op Bank and The Body Shop are good examples of how they have been able to **differentiate** themselves from the competition.

The momentum of such argument is now so great that the notion of social responsibility has become almost inextricably confused with the matter of ethics. The distinction of which is: ethics is more concerned with **absolute standards** of **right and wrong** and how conduct should be judged to be good or bad. It is about how we should live our lives and, in particular how we should behave towards others. It is therefore relevant to all forms of human activity. However, human nature being what it is, individuals have widely diverging views on what those standards should be. Inevitably, ethical conduct is therefore a matter of continuing debate as is the argument against corporate social responsibility.

From a **corporate view** *Milton Friedman* argues that:

- Businesses do not have responsibilities, only people have responsibilities. Managers in charge of organisations are responsible to the owners of the business, by whom they are employed.

- Employers may have charity as their aim, but generally it will be to make as much profit as possible while conforming to the basic rules of the society, both those embodied in law and those embodied in ethical custom.

- If the statement that a manager has social responsibilities is to have any meaning, it must mean that he is to act in some way that is not in the interest of his employers.

- If managers do this they are, generally speaking, spending the owner's money for purposes other than those they have been authorised; sometimes it is the money of customers or suppliers that is spent and, on occasion, the money of employees. By doing this, the manager is, in effect, both raising taxes and deciding how they should be spent, which are functions of government, not of business. There are two objections to this:

    (i) Managers have not been democratically elected or selected in any other way to exercise government power.

    (ii) Managers are not experts in government policy and cannot foresee the detailed effect of such social responsibility spending.

Friedman also argues that the social responsibility model is politically collectivist in nature and deplores the possibility that collectivism should be extended any further than absolutely necessary in a free society.

A second argument against the assumption of CSR is that the maximisation of wealth is the best way that society can benefit from a business's activities as outlined below.

- Maximising wealth has the effect of increasing tax revenues available to the state to disperse on socially desirable objectives.
- Maximising shareholder value has a 'trickle-down' down effect on other disadvantaged members of society.
- Many company shares are owned by pension funds, whose ultimate beneficiaries may not be the wealthy anyway.

From the **stakeholder view** is that many groups have a stake in what the organisation does. This is particularly important in the business context, where shareholders own the business but employees, customers and government also have particularly strong claims to having their interests considered. This is fundamentally an argument derived from **natural law theory** and is based on the notion of individual and **collective rights**.

It is suggested that modern organisations are so powerful, socially, economically and politically, that unrestrained use of their power will inevitably damage other people's rights. For example, they may blight an entire community by closing down a major facility, thus enforcing long-term unemployment of the local workforce. Similarly, they may damage people's quality of life by polluting the environment eg Union Carbide (Bhopal). They may use their purchasing power or market share to impose unequal contracts on suppliers and customers alike and may also exercise undesirable influence of government through their investment decisions. Under this approach, the exercise of CSR constrains the organisation to act at all times as a good citizen.

Another argument points out that organisations exist within society and are dependent upon it for the resources they use. Some of these resources are obtained by direct contracts with suppliers and others are not, being provided by government expenditure. Examples are: transport infrastructure, technical research and education for the workforce. Clearly, organisations contribute to the taxes that pay for these things, but the relationship is rather tenuous and the tax burden can be minimised by careful management eg Enron.

The implication is that organisations should recognise and pay for the facilities that society provides by means of socially responsible policies and actions.

(b) 2.0 **Becoming socially responsible**

CSR focuses on **how the organisation operates** rather than what is produced or the services provided. It encompasses environmental practices, how they relate to the communities in which they operate, their customers and suppliers and the way in which they are run internally.

Guidelines include **commitments** to which the organisations can sign up, **standards** to which they can adhere and models of good practice eg The Ethical Trading Initiative.

For example, The Global Sullivan Principles objective is to support economic social and political justice by companies. It supports human rights and equality of employment, including diversity, and aims to improve quality of life for the whole community. Their principles include:

- Equal opportunity of employment and freedom of association
- Providing **opportunities** to improve skills and capabilities for workers
- Health and safety at work
- Promoting sustainable environmental development

- Anti-corruption, promoting fair competition
- Providing training opportunities for disadvantaged people

Numerous independent professional bodies eg UN Global Compact, have also issued guidelines with regard to CSR. However, there is a risk for the organisation to go 'horribly wrong' if it tries to 'bolt on' a set of guidelines rather than finding one that suits the strategy and integrating it into organisational practices.

The UN Global Compact guidelines eg differ from those above in the following way.

- The avoidance of corporate human rights abuses
- Freedom of association and collective bargaining
- The elimination of forced labour and of child labour
- The elimination of employment discrimination
- Greater environmental responsibility initiatives
- The use of environmentally friendly technologies

Identifying the right guidelines and implementing is a tough process and needs to great commitment from the Board. Failure to adhere to guidelines may not deliver the competitive edge the organisation is looking for. For example, as Nike found, there was a deterioration of performance partly as a result of the customers' perception that the organisation mistreated factory workers.

(c) 3.0 **Ethical dilemmas**

There are a number of areas in which the various approaches to ethics and conflicting views of a organisation's responsibilities can create ethical dilemmas. These can **impact at the highest level**, affecting the development of policy, or lower down the hierarchy, especially if policy is unclear and guidance from more senior people is unavailable.

Dealing with unpleasantly **authoritarian governments** can be supported on the grounds that it contributes to economic growth and prosperity and all the benefits they bring to society in both countries concerned. On the other hand it can be opposed on the grounds as contributing to a fundamentally repugnant regime.

Honesty and advertising is an important problem. Many products are promoted exclusively on image. Deliberately creating the impression that purchasing a particular product will enhance their happiness, success and sex appeal of the buyer can be attacked as dishonest. It can be defended on the grounds that the supplier is actually selling a fantasy of dream rather than a physical article.

Dealing with employees is a contentious issued due to the opposing views of corporate responsibility and individual rights. The idea of a job as property to be defended has now disappeared from UK labour relations, but there is no doubt that corporate decisions that lead to redundancies are still deplored. This is because of the obvious impact of sudden unemployment on aspirations and living standards, even when the employment market is buoyant. Nevertheless, it is only proper for businesses to consider the cost of employing labour as well as its productive capacity. Even employers who accept that their employees' skills are their most important source of **competitive advantage** can be reduced to **cost cutting** in order to survive in lean times.

Another ethical problem concerns **payments by organisations to officials** who have the power to help or hinder the payers' operations. The fine distinction that exists in this area, is highlighted by *Walton*.

- **Extortion** – Foreign officials have been known to threaten organisations with the complete closure of local operations unless suitable payments are made.

- **Bribery** – This is payment for services of which an organisation is not legally entitled. There are some fine distinctions to be drawn eg some managers regard political contributions as bribery.

- **Grease money** – Multi-national organisations are sometimes unable to obtain services to which they are legally entitled because of deliberate stalling by local officials. Cash payments to the right people may then be enough to 'oil the machinery' of bureaucracy.

- **Gifts** – In some cultures eg Japan, gifts are regarded as an essential part of civilized negotiation, even in circumstances where to Western eyes they might appear ethically dubious. Managers operating in such a culture may feel at liberty to adopt the local customs.

Business ethics are also relevant to competitor behaviour. This is because a market can only be free if competition is fair. An example is the dispute between British Airways and Virgin that centred on issues of business ethics. This case suggests there is a distinction between competing aggressively and competing unethically.

Specimen paper

Managing Marketing Performance

Test Paper: Specimen paper

3 Hours Duration

> This examination is in two sections.
>
> **Part A** is compulsory and worth 50% of total marks.
>
> **Part B** has four questions, select two. Each answer will be worth 25% of total marks.
>
> **DO NOT** repeat the question in your answer but show clearly the number of the question attempted.

DO NOT OPEN THIS PAPER UNTIL YOU ARE READY TO
START UNDER EXAMINATION CONDITIONS

1 Mercer and Son

You have recently been appointed marketing manager for Mercer and Son.

Mercer and Son is a medium-sized food processing business. It had its origins in the late 1940s when the founder, John Mercer, opened a butcher's shop. Over the years his pies and baked products, originally prepared at home by his wife, became very popular and were certainly more profitable. When his son James joined the business this was the stimulus to expand the business into what it has become today. The company now employs about 300 people and produces a wide range of meat based pies and quiches, some delicatessen products and more recently ready-prepared meals. Expansion into the ready-prepared meals sector was key to gaining access to major supermarket retailers. Although relatively small by food industry standards the company has a high reputation and a well-respected brand for its pie and quiche products, although the ready-prepared meals are sold under supermarket own-labels.

After seeing the company through many years of continual growth and expansion into the major retail chains, James Mercer felt that it was time for him to retire and bring in a professional management team with the skills and capabilities to continue to grow the business. The new managing director was appointed about a year ago and one of his first tasks was to recruit a senior management team to support his ideas for growth. New members of the team include the production director, promoted from his previous role as factory manager, together with yourself, an accomplished and professional marketer recruited with a background in branded personal care products and insight and experience in dealing with retailers.

Although the business has grown substantially in recent years the new managing director has identified a number of areas of concern. The traditional strength of the company is its reputation for high-quality products, derived from the use of high quality meats and care and attention to production and manufacturing processes. However, it is apparent that the branded pie and quiche business is showing a flattening or even decline in sales, with delicatessen products being outclassed by cheaper and/or superior products particularly from France and Italy. This has been compensated for by the growth in the ready meals business but increasing price pressure from supermarkets is beginning to affect profitability, and their payment policies are affecting cash flow. As supermarkets influence a greater share of the product mix then this could become even more of a problem. The managing director is also aware, despite these problems, of his need to continue the growth of the business in order to achieve his objectives and meet shareholder expectations.

At the recent management meeting discussions were long and became very heated. In your report to the board and subsequent discussion you outlined several opportunities for growth; these included developing new, branded products to provide some protection from downward price pressure and to build on the traditional values of the company, and also to move into the 'foodservice' sector building on the capabilities of the company to produce ready meals in large quantities to high standards. The foodservice area would involve supplying institutions such as schools and hospitals with their meal requirements, but this would also require exceptionally high service and quality levels but would at least mean that the company was less dependent on retailers. The production director commented that the layout of the factory would need to be changed to accommodate short production runs and frequent line changes to meet the varying menu requirements.

The management team also discussed a recent, unexpected and unwelcome turn of events. There have been some recent reports in the media about high levels of bacterial contamination associated with certain meat products. The supermarket buyers had already contacted the company for assurances concerning the quality of product, and there was even talk of a formal inspection and audit. In addition, an environmental pressure group had suggested that the underlying cause of this was associated with 'factory farming' techniques, causing stress and ill health in the animals concerned with consequent concern for their welfare. You questioned the production director closely as to his sourcing policy, and expressed your concern that maybe corners were being cut in order to maintain margins despite the stated 'welfare friendly' policy. He was clearly indignant and offended that a new recruit, 'merely a marketing person used to selling shampoo and hairspray', should even dare to question the quality of the product. In fact, the meeting became quite heated as the management team realised that not only were the long-term prospects for the business rather challenging, but there was also the threat of a short-term emergency generated by the possibility of a food scare.

Realising that little further progress could be made, the managing director closed the meeting, commenting that he would meet each manager individually to discuss the issues relevant to them and what priorities should be decided.

PART A

Question 1

Following the management meeting the managing director has asked you to prepare a memorandum that addresses the following points:

(a) There is an **urgent need to deal with the threat** posed by the meat contamination issue. The managing director has asked for your **proposals** on how you might **respond to the threat** posed by the meat contamination issue, paying particular attention to the **priorities for action** with respect to the groups involved. (25 marks)

(b) The company can only afford to fund **one development opportunity**. Prepare a brief summary of the **advantages and disadvantages** of investing in additional **branded products versus entering the foodservice sector** and identify the **best opportunity**. Discuss how you would propose to progress the opportunity you have selected. (25 marks)

(50 marks in total)

PART B (Answer TWO questions only)

Question Two

In the mini case in Part A, the production director at Mercer and Son **reacted strongly** being questioned by the marketing managers. Discuss and explain how **different functional interests** within an organisation can be **aligned**.

(25 marks)

Question Three

With respect to the Mercer and Son mini-case study, the managing director has suggested that you need to **recruit a product manager** to assist in the work involved in expanding the business. He has asked you to prepare a business case to **justify the role**.

(25 marks)

Question Four

How might the **balanced scorecard** for a service business such as a **call centre**, differ from that of a **high volume component manufacturing business**, and why?

(25 marks)

Question Five

Explain how **service quality standards** might be initially set and subsequently maintained for the **after sales service of a manufacturer** of consumer electrical goods such as washing machines, dishwashers and vacuum cleaners.

(25 marks)

Suggested answers

DO NOT TURN THIS PAGE UNTIL YOU
HAVE COMPLETED THE TEST PAPER

Specimen paper: answers

1

MERCER AND SON

MEMORANDUM

To: Matthew Parks, Managing Director
From: Rhys David, Marketing Manager
Date: 28th July 20X4

Following our meeting the information you requested is set out below.

(a) **Meat contamination threat**

An outbreak of bacterial contamination of meat can cause negative publicity. Such unfavourable publicity can arise overnight and escalate dramatically. A single negative event that produces such publicity can wipe out the company's efforts and irreparably damage consumer attitudes.

Obviously, negative publicity is to be avoided at all costs. As a long-standing business with over 60 years' experience, the company's high reputation is at risk unless a **proactive** approach is adopted to avert this potential crisis. This involves **effective communication** between the company and its stakeholders concerning any future crisis. The company therefore may have to engage the services of a Public Relations (PR) Consultant. Due to the seriousness of this bacterial outbreak there is an urgent need to formulate and implement a plan of action. This could take the form of:

- Managing director informing the staff of the potential for a localised bacterial outbreak and the relevant plan of action. As an outbreak could seriously damage the reputation of the company, the employee livelihoods are at risk. By informing them, they become part of the team to help prevent any possibility of contamination or rumours.

- Visit the sources of meat supply making sure that they are maintaining stringent health and hygiene standards in their place of operation and are conforming to all Government regulations. Any doubts, and the company must consider re-sourcing suppliers.

- Internally, it would be advisable for the production director to make stringent checks on all meat handling procedures and known bacterial 'hot spots'. While the company has a good record for health and hygiene, publicly it must be seen to be 'squeaky' clean. Therefore, there may be a need to employ the services of a specialised agency to advise on prevention and eradication of any likely bacterial contamination.

Once the company has evidence of a 'clean bill of health' for all its operations, this will need to be communicated in order to meet stakeholders differing objectives. The objectives may be as follows.

- **Supermarkets** – To maintain and develop good working relationships between the two organisations to **meet customer demand for quality and value**.

- To achieve this during a possible crisis, Mercer and Son must continue to engage in open two-way communication about the situation. Factual evidence should be on hand for senior management to reassure the buyers and provide the opportunity for them to visit the premises. Furthermore, any suggestion of bacterial contamination from existing stock must be urgently investigated and stocks removed immediately if necessary. This is essential to maintain the objectives of Mercer and Son in its relationship with the supermarkets.

- **Employees** – To **maintain and improve levels of motivation** throughout the workforce through **effective two-way communication**.

    As with any organisation, employees must feel valued within to ensure that they continue to be motivated. In this instance this means keeping them up to date with all developments and also listening to what they have to say in response. Ideally, they may come up with some radical solutions that could be implemented in the future. This can be achieved through a variety of means eg meetings, newsletters, intranet, notice boards etc.

- **Suppliers** – Maintain and develop good working relationships.

    It is essential under the circumstances that open, honest and frank two-communication is conducted not only for the present but, for the future. This approach could be through senior management, sales staff, extranet and other customer facing personnel.

- **Consumer** – To **maintain high quality brand values**.

    It is very important for the future success of the company that we maintain the high quality and relationship between our brands and the consumer. Therefore, it would be appropriate to invest in a promotional campaign to reassure the consumer of the high quality food products and value. This campaign should include advertising, promotional offers and public relations activity (eg press releases, articles in magazines etc.) It may be necessary to offer a short-term contract to a PR Consultant to advise and conduct a PR campaign aimed at the differing stakeholder needs.

- **Environmental pressure groups and media** – To develop a **non-antagonistic relationship**.

    The PR Consultant should endeavour to build a friendly and approachable relationship with both groups and understand each one's needs. The approach however, should be proactive to avoid misinformation that can lead to unfavourable and destructive publicity.

This situation has highlighted the need for a crisis plan to be drawn up which should be led by a crisis management team. A set of **policies and procedures** must be implemented and made known to all employees within the organisation. The crisis team will meet regularly to review and update procedures particularly in the light of personnel changes and media and other stakeholder contacts.

(b) **Branded products vs the foodservice sector**

Results at Mercer and Son have shown a **flattening or slight decline in sales** in the core products of branded pies and quiches. On the other hand, there has been a growth in the ready meal business under supermarket own brand labels. Increased price pressure from supermarkets is affecting profitability and their payment policies are affecting cash flow. In light of the above, the managing director is aware that the business needs to grow in order to achieve the objectives and meet shareholder expectations. As a result of the current financial situation there is only sufficient funds to support the development of one opportunity. This could either be an additional branded product or entering the food service sector. It is therefore essential to evaluate the potential for each before proceeding.

Advantages and disadvantages

A table showing some of the advantages and disadvantages for additional branded products and entering the food service sector is shown below.

Additional branded product	
Advantages	**Disadvantages**
Possibility of economies of scale.	The new brand could fail and adversely affect the core brand.
Less risky because customer expectations have already been built up with the core brand (pies and quiches).	Excessive extension can dilute the values of the brand.
Production costs should be able to fit in with existing production line although some small adaptations may need to be made.	The new brand must stand on its own and therefore must be differentiated from competition.
Support for existing brand through promotional activities eg buy existing brand and try new brand at half price.	Due to customer perceptions that quality brands command higher prices, customers may not accept quality and traditional values at lower prices.
Gain supermarket shelf space dominance offering a wider choice for existing and new customers.	Flattening out and declining market.
Increase product mix thus widening the base and providing further opportunity for future growth.	Price pressure from supermarkets and payment policy affecting company cash flow.
Food service sector	
Growth in the ready meals market.	Increased capital expenditure for potential changes to production.
Less dependent on the retail sector.	New skills required for selling and production line.
Good reputation already in existence.	
Producing supermarket own brand labels for ready prepared meals does not risk the company reputation.	Cost of training/re-training and quality control due to the exceptionally high levels of quality and service required for the sector.
New market area offering huge potential for company growth.	Disruption to existing production lines to re-organise and accommodate proposed changes.
Not subjected to overseas competition.	

The best opportunity

Before making a decision due consideration must be given to all the advantages and disadvantages of both proposals. There will be champions for each proposal. However, the final choice should be made with a view that **long-term growth and profitability** are the objectives of Mercer and Son to meet stakeholder expectations. As a result of this, the opinion is held that the food service sector offers the best opportunity.

The reasons for making this choice are based on the fact that:

- At present there is little growth within the current branded products market unlike the food service sector which is currently experiencing growth.

- While there is **increased competition** from abroad for delicatessen products both on price and quality against the Company's own brands, in the UK food service sector, there is less international competition and a trend for hospitals, schools and other institutions to outsource provision of readymade meals. This reflects growth in the market.

- Due to the **cost implications** of transportation and specialised menus for hospitals, for example, it may be cheaper to source locally than from abroad.

- By introducing a new brand to the product range it will have to fight for shelf space within an already crowded market. In the food service sector there is no competition for shelf space only to produce high quality ready meals that are **value for money**.

- There are currently price pressures and payment policies from supermarkets that are affecting Mercer and Son's cash flow. It is hoped by moving into the food service sector that will be some improvement in payment policies as hospitals and schools are part of the Public Sector. However, competition will have to be faced and only when our first tenders for business have been placed will we know how competitive the market is.

- Introducing another branded product into the retail sector will further unbalance the product mix in the retail sector making the company more vulnerable as a result ie there is a need to avoid 'putting all the eggs in one basket'. By diversifying into the food service sector this will give Mercer and Son a more **balanced product mix**.

Proposed progress

Thorough **marketing research** must be carried out within the food service sector, including an internal and external audit. These results should indicate some of the following.

Internal audit:

- **Ability and capability of existing sales department** to meet the new challenges or whether there is a need to employ new staff with eg relevant food service experience.

- Further **training needs and development** for current sales and production staff.

- **Production and distribution capabilities** to meet the new demands.

- **Capital investment** required for eg changes to production lines, increased distribution and new staff.

External audit:

- State of competition and market ie **market attractiveness** and whether there is a big enough market for the intended development.

- **Government legislation** (health and safety certification, food labelling, competitive tendering etc) regulating this particular sector.

With a thorough understanding of the analysis of the results, strategic planning can take place accommodating all the relevant opportunities and challenges. It will be up to management to develop, implement and control the **strategic plan** taking corrective action where necessary in order to meet company objectives and stakeholder expectations.

2

Background

Faced with the threat of bacterial contamination in the production plant can only be a very stressful time for, in particular, a production director. Such stress may cause tempers to flare and insecurities to arise. These insecurities may also be borne from the fact that the production director was formerly the production manager and inwardly focused on the quality of the product. This is referred to as being **product orientated**. Thus his focus was not on the external customer's needs as was the marketing manager's but purely on the quality of the product supplied. The marketing manager has the customer at the centre of the organisation, a concept known as **marketing orientation**.

Conflict

The expressed concerns that corners were being cut in order to maintain margins despite the stated 'welfare friendly' policy was possibly seen as being undermined. This brought about a feeling of indignation and caused a heated exchange of words. If both employees were part of an organisation that was marketing orientated then both would have seen this challenge from the customer's point of view and therefore little reason for conflict.

The production director may also have perceived that there was **inter-functional conflict** thinking that one function was trying to increase power at the expense of the other. This may have been reflected in the comment that the new marketing manager was 'merely a marketing person selling shampoo and hairspray and how dare he question the quality of the product'.

Overcoming conflict

One way of overcoming such conflict is to implement an **internal marketing concept** which can be defined as: 'aligning, educating and motivating staff towards institutional objectives the process by which personnel understand and recognise not only the value of the programme but their place in it' (*Winter*). In view of this, the organisation needs to address **cross-functional co-ordination**. *Glassman and MacAfee* suggest this can be achieved by some of the following.

- **Shared information systems** that can increase the speed and flow of information between functions and help to build trust and thereby reduce the areas of inter-functional conflict

- Introducing **cross-functional teams** as they have been found to the most successful integrating mechanism

- **Involving representatives** from personnel or other functions onto marketing committees and *visa versa*

- **Creating liaison** by appointing individuals within functions whose role is to communicate with other departments regarding any action or policies that may impact on each other

By adopting these practices it can create knowledge in new ways, increase sharing of information and capability to respond more rapidly to changes in the market. Given the nature of inter-functional rivalry and the potential for conflict, internal marketing cannot and should not be the sole responsibility of any department but needs to come from strategic management (*Ahmed and Rafiq*).

Internal marketing programmes should not be implemented in a vacuum. Effective implementation requires a **supportive environment**. Senior management should be responsible for transmitting values through the organisation of a customer orientation and other values associated with internal marketing, and in particular **effective communication**.

A Process of Development

As the management team is newly appointed they too are going through a **process of development** described by *Tuckman* as:

- Forming – A stage of initial orientation and interpersonal testing
- Storming – A stage of conflict over tasks and working as a team
- Norming – A stage of consolidation around task and operating agendas
- Performing – A stage of teamwork and focused task performance
- Adjourning – A stage of task completion and disengagement

From the information so far it would appear that this team is still at the storming stage and thus are experiencing some hostility and in-fighting and are therefore less likely to be functioning effectively. It is the role of the managing director who is in the process of putting the team together to:

- Promote a strong vision of what the team can achieve
- Identify the stages the team are going through until they are fully able to perform (patience is of the order and not to despair)
- Facilitate the development of and commitment to a team vision
- Provide initial direction and then gradually let go as team members' confidence begins to grow
- Facilitate the development of mutual trust and support
- Encourage interaction through genuine collaboration (working together)
- Encourage commitment to mutual team success as well as individual success
- Help the team to work towards preventing and learning from mistakes, not just correcting them later

Conclusion

Implementation of some of the above measures may well have avoided a conflict of interest between the marketing manager and production director as well as establishing a more harmonious team.

3

MERCER AND SON

To: Charles Lawrence, Managing Director
From: James Bell, Marketing Manager
Subject: Product Manager Recruitment
Date: 7th August 20X4

1.0 Justification of the role

Due to the expanding nature of the business and our desire to meet company growth objectives and shareholder expectations, coupled with the decision to expand the business into the Food Service Sector, there is a need to employ a product manager because the work of the team will be expanding. Until the present time Mercer and Son has only worked within the Private Sector. The Public Sector however is an untapped market as far as this company is concerned. With the Government legislation an competitive tendering it is advisable that the company has on board a person who has **expertise and understands the specialist nature of the business**. This will be **complementary** to existing skills in the branded goods sector.

On a cautionary note, should the established team attempt to undertake the responsibilities involved in diversifying into the Food Service Sector, our current knowledge of producing quality ready meals may delude us into thinking that the skills needed for dealing with the Public Sector will be the same. Furthermore, there will be no one person responsible for this new project and sharing responsibilities dramatically increases the **risk of failure**.

The recommendation therefore is to see the addition of a product manager as a **long-term investment** to help grow the business and meet company objectives and shareholder expectations. This report further sets out to discuss the recruitment process and the person specification.

2.0 Expanding the team

A **systematic approach** needs to be adopted as recruitment and selection can be costly and time consuming. Due to the specialist nature of the role, the aim should be to 'get the right person' and 'get the person right'. This means following a planned recruitment process that will provide the company with the best talent, consistent with the needs of the business and its capacity to make full use of the person that it has recruited. Below is a diagram showing the recruitment chain.

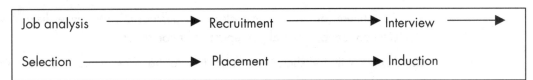

3.0 The recruitment process

- **Job analysis** - When selecting a new employee the first step as shown above is to prepare a job analysis.

    The Chartered Institute of Personnel and Development's (CIPD) Recruitment Code of Practice states that all recruitment **must** begin with a **Job Description** which is the job's component tasks, duties, objectives and standard and/or a **Person Specification** which describes the skills knowledge and qualities needed to do the job (CIPD, 1995:18). This **person-orientated approach** focuses on the generic qualities and behaviour required by our organisation and **offers a flexible approach**.

- **Recruitment** – Our company is characterised by a **culture** that respects:
    - Individuality
    - Encourages communication and teamwork
    - Rewards achievement by offering a high standard in terms of personal and career development opportunities.

    The decision needs to be made whether the right person can be found **'in-house'** or whether to look for **'new blood'**. If recruiting through advertising in the media, for example, adverts should be placed for at least three editions in order to maximise the response and minimise the risk of selecting the wrong candidate. Recruitment can also be carried out through selected agencies. Each responding candidate must be provided with an application pack that includes :-

- A Job Description
- A Person Specification
- An Application Form
- An Equal Opportunities Policy
- A Company Information Sheet

The **description of the Company** shows the strategy and culture of our organisation. This is also a means of communication in attracting the 'right' person to the job. The **job location, pay, essential requirements** and how to apply should also be specified. The advertisement must be **non-discriminatory** on grounds of sex, race or disabilities.

- **Interview and selection**
    - Matching the person to the person specification can be done through **assessment** of a presentation that should be **based on the Company Interview Appraisal System**. Assessment will be based on the following:
    - Personal Qualities and Skills
    - Acquired Knowledge or Qualifications
    - Innate abilities (how candidates present themselves during the interview).
    - Motivation
    - Adjustment (ability to demonstrate eg persuasion; resilience; flexibility; realism; self confidence; mental perception; self control etc)

    Candidates will be short-listed from this to go forward for the next step in the process.

- **Placement and induction**

    An offer can be made during a meeting wherein the **salary, additional benefits, working hours, terms and conditions** (including six month probationary period to protect both parties) and **starting date** will be agreed. Induction can be carried out on the first day.

4.0 Person Specification

The **Person Specification** can be taken as the basis for outlining the essential and desirable qualities required to carry out this job. Candidates should demonstrate:-

- The **ability to communicate** – Show good presentation skills, clarity and effectiveness, make use of active listening skills and demonstrate honesty. This quality is essential in dealing with internal matters and institutions and public sector organisations.

- Ability to **manage change** – Show positive response to change and show ability to implement change.

- Ability to **manage self** – Show flexibility, adaptability and have pride and persistence in achieving objectives, goals and tasks.

- Ability to **work with people** – Show ability to build and maintain working relationships, both within a team and cross functionally in the achievement of their individual and team goals.

- Ability to **be analytical** – Show evidence of strategic thinking and a good understanding of budgetary analysis.

4

Introduction

To understand how the **balanced scorecard** for a service business such as a call centre can differ from that of a high volume component manufacturing business, there is a need to first understand the complexities of *Kaplan and Norton's* balanced scorecard. It is a technique designed to ensure that the **different functions of the business are integrated together** in order that they work to achieve the corporate goals. The system can give a fast but comprehensive view of the business by measuring current performance that is used to target future performance. It is these operational measures that are the **drivers of future financial performance**. It covers four main categories: **customer knowledge, internal business processes, financial performance, learning and growth** while also providing a means to measure the organisation's **innovation and improvement activities**. Kaplan and Norton suggest that the balanced scorecard can take companies beyond the conventional yardsticks of sales, profit and cash flow. However, this can only be done if companies meet their set objectives.

Performance measures

Objective setting is not an isolated process. There is a clear link between setting objectives and the setting of **performance measures** thus managers have a need to know the key criteria by which their performance against objectives will be measured. While traditional financial accounting measures like return on investment and earnings per share can give misleading signals for **continuous improvement** and innovation, the balanced scorecard allows managers to look at the business from four important perspectives as discussed below.

Drummond and Ensor suggest at the core of the balanced scorecard approach is the belief that managers have to be able to look at a business from these perspectives as follows.

- **Customer perspective** – Customers' perception of a business is critical, and financial measures alone do not always provide a true reflection. Customers are generally concerned with quality; service; performance and time therefore an organisation should develop objectives and performance measures for each of these categories looking from the customer perspective over time.

- **Internal perspective** – Critical internal processes have to be identified by managers that will allow them to satisfy customer needs. By identifying the processes that are important to customer satisfaction, managers are able to identify the functions and competencies in which they need to excel.

- **Innovation and learning perspective** - An organisation's ability to create value is inextricably linked to its capacity to continually improve through innovation and learning.

- **Financial perspective** – This enables organisations to view the business from the shareholders' point of view. The success of the financial performance is measured on an organisation's strategy and implementation.

The balanced scorecard provides managers with a **wider view** of the business rather than concentrating purely on financial criteria. The organisation has to create distinct objectives for each of these perspectives and at the same time develop the accompanying performance measures. While it is a means of ensuring consistency between objectives, it is also a process that forces managers to understand many **complex relationships** and to overcome some of the traditional functional barriers common to **strategic development**.

Call centre vs high volume component manufacturing business

A balanced scorecard will undoubtedly differ between a call centre and a high volume component manufacturing business because the approach for a call centre would be through a customer perspective and the approach for a component manufacturing business would be through an internal perspective.

- **Call centre** (customer perspective) – Company strategic objectives will be set to offer the **customer value for money**, **customer satisfaction** and a **competitive price**. Performance can be strategically measured through a customer ranking survey, pricing index, customer satisfaction index and a mystery caller index, for example.

- **High volume component manufacturing business** (internal perspective) – This type of business involves setting strategic objectives for **marketing** of product and service development and to shape customer requirements. There is a need to lower **manufacturing** costs and improve **project management**. Logistics require a strategic approach in order to **reduce delivery costs** and there is a need for **inventory management**. **Quality** is key to the approach. Performance can be strategically measured through: pioneer percentage of product portfolio; hours with customer on new work; total expenses per unit vs. competition; safety incident index; delivered cost per unit; inventory level compared to plan and output rate and the need to re-work.

5

Introduction

A **service** can be defined as: **deeds, processes and performances**. It is an **intangible product** that cannot be stored or physically possessed. With the increase in market competition, customer expectations and the effects of consumerism, it is therefore important to strive to get the quality of service right the first time as a customer's perception is formed in a matter of seconds (**moments of truth**) of a service encounter.

Setting standards

Service quality standards must therefore be set and subsequently maintained for the after sales service of, for example, a manufacturer of household 'white' goods. However, unlike manufacturers whose **quality control procedures** should be sufficient to satisfy the customer with the quality and distribution of goods, a service is much more complex because of the **people factor**. The implications have made the four Ps - price; place; promotion; product - in marketing inadequate. For services, the addition of people, process and physical evidence needed to be introduced to cater for the service element of an organisation. For example, services are provided by **people** for people and usually provided in a number of sequential steps. This **process** can be spoiled or enhanced at any step in the sequence and the **physical evidence** can be a maker or spoiler of experience of the service.

Management time and resources must be allocated to **set and control quality** of the service, as it is a significant basis that customers use for differentiating between competing services. Quality is also a key contributor to **bottom line profit performance** and can only be defined by customers. Standards can be set by :–

- Fully understanding customer expectations.
- Outlining specific service quality criteria
- Benchmarking against industry standards
- Monitoring the delivery of service
- Monitoring employee performance and motivation and implementing remedial action if necessary
- Management of control operations

Customer expectations also serve as standards against which subsequent service experiences are compared and if service performance falls short of expectations, dissatisfaction occurs. Researchers have found that consumers consider at least five dimensions in their assessments of service quality. These dimensions represent how consumers organise information about service quality in their minds. Research has found it particularly relevant in the appliance and repair maintenance, insurance and banking sectors. These dimensions are:

- **Reliability** – Ability to perform the promised service dependably and accurately eg problem fixed first time
- **Responsiveness** – Willingness to help customers and provide prompt service eg no long waits on the phone for appliance information or service engineer
- **Assurance** – Employees' knowledge and courtesy and their ability to inspire trust and confidence eg knowledgeable sales staff and quality engineers
- **Empathy** – Caring, individualised attention given to a customer eg addresses customer by name and remembers any previous problem
- **Tangibles** – Appearance of physical facilities, equipment, personnel, and written materials eg the uniform of the sales staff and engineer as well as the equipment used to do the job

Maintaining service quality

Providing high quality service on a consistent basis is very difficult. However, measures such as the use of the **'SERVQUAL'** survey utilising the five dimensions listed above will enable the organisation to maintain and improve service quality. This survey is based on a graded scale from strongly agree to strongly disagree across all the dimensions. Once an organisation knows how it is performing on each of the dimensions of service quality, it can use a number of methods to try to maintain and improve its quality. These are:

- **Development** of customer orientated mission statement and clear senior management support for quality improvement initiatives
- **Regular customer satisfaction research** including customer surveys and panels, mystery shoppers, analysis of complaints and similar industry studies for benchmarking purposes
- **Setting and monitoring standards and communicating results**
- Establishments of **systems for customer complaints and feedback**
- **Encouragement of employee participation** often through the use of quality circles and project teams
- **Rewarding** excellent service

Advantages to the organisation

There are two ways an organisation can gain from improving their quality of service.

- **Higher sales revenues** and **improved marketing effectiveness** brought about by improved customer retention, positive word-of-mouth recommendations and the ability to increase prices

- **Improved productivity and reduced costs** because there is less re-work, higher employee morale and lower employee turnover

Topic index

Topic index

Balanced scorecard, 10, 93
Benchmarking, 87
Brand strategies, 6, 59
Brand stretching, 5, 46
Brand, 46
Brands, 56
Budget, 69
Budgeting, 10, 95
Building, 102
Business process re-engineering (BPR), 87

Change and the individual, 4, 44
Change, 4, 40
Codes of ethical standards, 48
Coercion, 49
Conferences, 7, 71
Corporate social responsibility, 23, 62
Creative people, 8, 75
Creativity, 8, 72
Crisis, 5, 52
Customer perspective, 93

Definition stage, 71
Direct marketing, 66

Emotional intelligence, 3, 37
Ethical dilemmas, 23, 132
Ethics, 6, 61, 62
Expenditure, 9, 89
Extended marketing mix, 51
Extranet, 66

Feedback and control system, 9
Feedback and control, 91
Financial perspective, 94
Functional interests, 140

Groupthink, 27

Heterogeneity, 51
Human resource planning, 81

Induction programme, 10
Innovation and learning perspective, 94
Innovation, 8, 72, 78
Inseparability, 51
Integrity, 5, 48
Integrity-based approach, 50
Internal business perspective, 93
Internal communication, 10

Internal communications plan, 10
Internal communications, 98

Key influences on ethical conduct, 48

Leadership and performance, 3, 35

Managing outside resources, 9
Market fragmentation, 39
Marketing audits, 92
Marketing orientation, 4, 42
Marketing skills, 81
Marketing task, 4, 39
Moments of Truth, 63
Motivation, 3, 28

New product development, 30

Outside resources, 9
Outsourcing, 8, 14, 77, 106

Participation, 3, 27
People, 51
Performance measurement indicator, 16
Perishability, 51
Personal amorality, 49
Personal selling, 66
Physical evidence, 51
PIMS (Profit Impact of Marketing Strategy), 90
Planning a team, 33
Planning for growth, 9, 81
Planning, 81
Point of purchase, 66
Processes, 51
Product development, 3
Profile, 66
Project management, 68
Project, 7, 71
Pull, 66
Push and pull, 6, 66
Push, 66

Quality management, 9, 86

Relationship marketing, 5, 9, 54, 86

Sales promotions, 67
Service quality, 6, 63, 64, 141
Services marketing, 50
Shareholder value analysis, 6, 58

159

Topic index

Shareholder value approach (SVA), 57
Social change, 39
Social responsibility, 6, 61
Stakeholder analysis, 15
Standard costing system, 70
Strategic control, 16, 112
Strategic management process, 16
Strategic management, 111
Suppliers, 9, 83

Teams, 28, 100

Technological innovation, 39
Timescale, 69
Total quality management (TQM), 67, 88
Training, 101
Types of outside marketing resources, 83

Value-based management, 59

Work/life balance, 37

See overleaf for information on other
BPP products and how to order

CIM Order

To BPP Professional Education, Aldine Place, London W12 8AA
Tel: 020 8740 2211. Fax: 020 8740 1184
email: publishing@bpp.com
online: www.bpp.com

Mr/Mrs/Ms (Full name) _____
Daytime delivery address _____
Postcode _____
Daytime Tel _____
Date of exam (month/year) _____

	2004 Texts		2004 Kits		Passcards	
PROFESSIONAL CERTIFICATE IN MARKETING						
1 Marketing Fundamentals	£19.95	☐	£9.95	☐	£6.95	☐
2 Marketing Environment	£19.95	☐	£9.95	☐	£6.95	☐
3 Customer Communications	£19.95	☐	£9.95	☐	£6.95	☐
4 Marketing in Practice	£19.95	☐	£9.95	☐	£6.95	☐
PROFESSIONAL DIPLOMA IN MARKETING						
5 Marketing Research and Information	£19.95	☐	£9.95	☐	£6.95	☐
6 Marketing Planning	£19.95	☐	£9.95	☐	£6.95	☐
7 Marketing Communications	£19.95	☐	£9.95	☐	£6.95	☐
8 Marketing Management in Practice	£19.95	☐	£9.95	☐	£6.95	☐
PROFESSIONAL POST-GRADUATE DIPLOMA IN MARKETING						
9 Analysis and Evaluation	£20.95	☐	£9.95	☐	£6.95	☐
10 Strategic Marketing Decisions	£20.95	☐	£9.95	☐	£6.95	☐
11 Managing Marketing Performance	£20.95	☐	£9.95	☐	£6.95	☐
12 Strategic Marketing in Practice	£26.95	☐	N/A		N/A	

SUBTOTAL £ _____

POSTAGE & PACKING

Study Texts and Kits

	First	Each extra	Online
UK	£5.00	£2.00	£2.00
Europe**	£6.00	£4.00	£4.00
Rest of world	£20.00	£10.00	£10.00

Passcards

	First	Each extra	Online
UK	£2.00	£1.00	£1.00
Europe**	£3.00	£2.00	£2.00
Rest of world	£8.00	£8.00	£8.00

Reduced postage rates apply if you **order online** at www.bpp.com

Grand Total (Cheques to *BPP Professional Education*) I enclose a cheque for (incl. Postage) £ _____

Or charge to Access/Visa/Switch

Card Number ☐☐☐☐ ☐☐☐☐ ☐☐☐☐ ☐☐☐☐

Expiry date _____ Start Date _____

Issue Number (Switch Only) _____

Signature _____

We aim to deliver to all UK addresses inside 5 working days. A signature will be required. Orders to all EU addresses should be delivered within 6 working days.

All other orders to overseas addresses should be delivered within 8 working days.

** Europe includes the Republic of Ireland and the Channel Islands.

CIM – Professional Post-graduate Diploma: Managing Marketing Performance (10/04)

REVIEW FORM & FREE PRIZE DRAW

All original review forms from the entire BPP range, completed with genuine comments, will be entered into one of two draws on 31 January 2005 and 31 July 2005. The names on the first four forms picked out on each occasion will be sent a cheque for £50.

Name: _____   Address: _____

_____

_____

How have you used this Kit?
(Tick one box only)
☐ Self study (book only)
☐ On a course: college_____
☐ Other _____

Why did you decide to purchase this Kit?
(Tick one box only)
☐ Have used companion Text
☐ Have used BPP Kits in the past
☐ Recommendation by friend/colleague
☐ Recommendation by a lecturer at college
☐ Saw advertising in journals
☐ Saw website
☐ Other _____

During the past six months do you recall seeing/receiving any of the following?
(Tick as many boxes as are relevant)
☐ Our advertisement in the *Marketing Success*
☐ Our advertisement in *Marketing Business*
☐ Our brochure with a letter through the post
☐ Our brochure with *Marketing Business*
☐ Saw website

Which (if any) aspects of our advertising do you find useful?
(Tick as many boxes as are relevant)
☐ Prices and publication dates of new editions
☐ Information on product content
☐ Facility to order books off-the-page
☐ None of the above

Have you used the companion Study Text for this subject?   ☐ Yes   ☐ No
Do you intend to use the new companion Passcards for this subject?   ☐ Yes   ☐ No

Your ratings, comments and suggestions would be appreciated on the following areas.

	Very useful	Useful	Not useful
Introductory section (Study advice, key question checklist etc)	☐	☐	☐
Exam standard questions	☐	☐	☐
Content of suggested answers	☐	☐	☐
Index	☐	☐	☐
Structure and presentation	☐	☐	☐

	Excellent	Good	Adequate	Poor
Overall opinion of this Kit	☐	☐	☐	☐

Do you intend to continue using BPP Study Texts/Kits/Passcards?   ☐ Yes   ☐ No

Please note any further comments and suggestions/errors on the reverse of this page.

Please return to: Glenn Haldane, BPP Professional Education, FREEPOST, London, W12 8BR

CIM – Professional Post-graduate Diploma: Managing Marketing Performance (10/04)

REVIEW FORM & FREE PRIZE DRAW (continued)

Please note any further comments and suggestions/errors below.

FREE PRIZE DRAW RULES

1 Closing date for 31 January 2005 draw is 31 December 2004. Closing date for 31 July 2005 draw is 30 June 2005.

2 Restricted to entries with UK and Eire addresses only. BPP employees, their families and business associates are excluded.

3 No purchase necessary. Entry forms are available upon request from BPP Professional Education. No more than one entry per title, per person. Draw restricted to persons aged 16 and over.

4 Winners will be notified by post and receive their cheques not later than 6 weeks after the relevant draw date. List of winners will be supplied on request.

5 The decision of the promoter in all matters is final and binding. No correspondence will be entered into.